NARROW GAUGE IN
SWEDEN & NORWAY

by James Waite

Published by Mainline & Maritime Ltd, 3 Broadleaze, Upper Seagry, near Chippenham, SN15 5EY
Tel: 07770 748615   www.mainlineandmaritime.co.uk   orders@mainlineandmaritime.co.uk
ISBN: 978-1-913797-13-3 Printed in the UK © Mainline & Maritime Ltd, & Author 2022

Front Cover: PRYDZ has almost completed the climb from Bingsfos and approaches Fossum station on the Tertitten Railway in Norway on 11 December 2010.
Back Cover: No 3147 arrives at Ankarsrum on the Smalspårsjärnvägen Hultsfred–Västervik, Sweden, on 11 July 2015.
Above: The Jädraås-Tallås Järnväg's No 4 crosses the River Jädraån near Tallås on 22 July 2006.

Sweden and Norway were late entrants to the railway age. Norway was first off the mark when a standard gauge line north from Oslo opened in 1854, built by a private company though with some government involvement. The country was politically a part of Sweden for most of the nineteenth century, although it enjoyed a considerable measure of self-government.

The first section of what became Sweden's mainline system opened two years later. The country had seen a number of false starts, encouraged by a decision that the railways should be built by private interests as had been the case in most of Europe. Eventually the lack of progress brought a change of direction and in order to kickstart construction the state decided it would build principal railways, something previously tried only in Belgium.

Local lines could still be promoted by private concerns, and included railways built to a surprising variety of gauges. Indeed the country's first railway, a 1,099mm one based at Frykstad, opened back in 1849, initially using horse traction. It served an iron mining and smelting district in western Bergslagen, to the north of Lake Vänern, the largest of Sweden's many lakes. It was followed by the Kristinehamns Järnväg, not far away, which opened the following year. In 1855 the Frykstad line bought a steam loco, only the second to run anywhere in the country. The Kristinehamn line's first loco arrived in 1857. Like many of Sweden's gauges 1,099mm looks odd when expressed in metric measurements, but this is not surprising since the country did not adopt the metric system until 1889. This one equates to 44 verktum or Swedish inches.

No more railways were built to the gauge. Four lines were built to the south of Lake Vänern in the late 1850's and early 1860's with a gauge of 1,217mm or four British feet. Its adoption reflected considerable British involvement in the early development of the country's railways and the supply of its locos. Over towards the east the Köping-Uttersbergs Järnväg opened in 1866. Its gauge of 1,093mm must have been the most unusual in the country. The line was intended to be 1,067mm or 3ft 6ins, again reflecting British influence. However its first locos were built in Sweden, and in an attempt to assist the railway specified that the gauge should be 3.59 Swedish feet. The builders decided that they could not possibly mean this as gauges were always expressed in British measurements, and they built them to 3.59 British feet, or 1,093mm instead. Fortunately the misunderstanding was discovered before much track had been laid, and the locos'

gauge was adopted for it.

Back in 1853 the Norbergs Järnväg was built with a gauge of 891mm (three Swedish feet). However trial runs with FÖRSTLINGEN, the country's first loco, were unsuccessful. Steam operation on so narrow a gauge was deemed impractical and before it opened the line was converted to 1,188mm gauge (four Swedish feet). There continued to be a demand in Bergslagen for a narrower gauge. The Kroppa Järnväg opened about the same time, initially as a horse-worked railway, but in the late 1860s it consulted no less a person than CE Spooner, the manager and engineer of the 60cm gauge Ffestiniog Railway, about introducing steam operation. He advised that it would be perfectly feasible provided the boiler pressure was sufficiently high to power the small cylinders which would be involved. There is some doubt about the line's gauge during its early years but by the early 1870s it was definitely 802mm, equal to 2.7 Swedish feet. Two locos were built for it by the nearby Kristinehamn factory which was run by Harald Asplund, a noted engineer.

He and Claes Adelsköld, another respected engineer who had designed both FÖRSTLINGEN and the loco at Frykstad, collaborated in the adoption of 802mm for several of Bergslagen's railways, and 222km of lines were built in all. The two subsequently fell out over patent rights for rear carrying axles. Mr Adelsköld's design involved a trailing radial axle which constrained the size of a conventional firebox on a very narrow gauge, while Mr Asplund's was mounted behind the firebox, reportedly inspired by the rear wheel fitted by Fletcher Jennings to the Talyllyn Railway's first loco. Thereafter Mr Adelsköld endorsed the use of 891mm to allow for a wider firebox. A significant event was the opening in 1873 of the Hjo-Stenstorps Järnväg; it was originally planned as another 802mm line but was built as the very first 891mm one instead. The gauge soon became popular. Altogether about 3,030km of 891mm lines were built and Sweden became for most purposes a mixed gauge country.

In addition to many isolated railways two large networks developed, one in Västergötland and one in Östergötland and Småland, separated only by the narrow Lake Vättern. For many years it was possible to travel on 891mm gauge trains all the way across the country, from Gothenburg in the west to several ports on the country's eastern coast, on a journey interrupted only by a ferry ride across the lake. There were, in addition, several isolated public railways in many parts of the country.

Exceptions to the gauge's widespread adoption included Bergslagen, which mostly remained faithful to 802mm, and the far southeast of Sweden where a network of about 600km of 1,067mm or 3ft 6ins gauge railways was built from 1874. One 3ft 6ins line reached across to the west coast at Halmstad, and another met up with the Östergötland and Småland 891mm network at both Torsås and Växjö. Curiously the network's loading gauge was lower than that of the 891mm gauge lines and some of its locos had a distinctly squat look.

Norway adopted the 3ft 6ins gauge for all those railways not expected to connect directly with Sweden's standard gauge system, the decision being guided by CA Pihl, the widely respected director and engineer of Norges Statsbaner or NSB, the state railway. The line from Hamar to Grundset was the world's first steam-worked 3ft 6ins railway when it opened in 1862. It was the earliest section of Rørosbanen which eventually reached Trondheim. Altogether 1,055km of state-owned 3ft 6ins lines were built. Some were isolated or were feeders to the standard gauge system. Others were distinctly main line in character; in addition to Rørosbanen they included a network to the west of Oslo and a smaller one on the south west coast between Stavanger, Egersund and Flekkefjord. A line to Torpshammar from Sundsvall, on Sweden's east coast 370km north of Stockholm, was also built to 3ft 6ins gauge as it was intended to meet up with Rørosbanen, though eventually the line east from Trondheim was built to standard gauge, and the Sundsvall section was soon converted. Within Sweden the railway is called Mittbanan.

600mm was the final addition to the gauges of Sweden's public railways. Seven were eventually built, mostly to serve small towns or impoverished districts thought unlikely to be able to support even an 891mm one. The first were closely associated with the development in France of Paul Decauville's portable 600mm gauge system. It attracted much international attention in the wake of the Great Exhibition held in Paris in 1889 to mark the centenary of the French Revolution. Along with the Eiffel Tower, the exhibition's most-loved attractions included a temporary 600mm gauge railway built by Decauville to promote his system. It was a brilliant publicity coup and its trains, worked by the world's first Mallet locos and some stylish carriages, had carried more than six million passengers by the time the exhibition closed. The first Swedish line, the Kosta-Lessebo Järnväg, ordered only the second of the Mallets to be built two years earlier when its manager, one Axel Hummel who was then only twenty eight years old, visited Decauville in Paris.

Norway had no public 600mm gauge railways, and the 750mm gauge Sulitjelmabanen, which opened in 1892, Nesttun-Osbanen, near Bergen, which followed two years later, and Urskog–Hølandsbanen which opened between 1896 and 1903, were the country's narrowest lines. Both countries also possessed many fascinating narrow gauge industrial systems; they included all the gauges used by the public railways plus others, and some which were used nowhere else.

All the Norwegian state-owned railways were merged into NSB in 1883, and in 1887 Statens Järnvägar, or SJ, was set up to operate the Swedish ones. In 1939 the Swedish parliament passed a law intended to bring all the country's public railways under state control but the process was gradual. In both countries some of the more prosperous narrow gauge lines, were later converted to standard gauge, but many followed the inevitable decline seen all over the world and eventually closed. Now only the 891mm gauge Roslagsbanan still sees commercial use; this busy electrified railway serves the suburbs to the north east of Stockholm and may soon be extended underground to the city centre. Fortunately sections of other lines which survived into the 1960s or later were rescued for preservation, thanks to the farsightedness of enthusiasts throughout the region. Norsk Jernbanemuseum, Norway's national railway museum at Hamar, was founded as long ago as 1896. Its Swedish equivalent, now called just Järnvägmuseet, followed in 1915, based initially at Stockholm and since 1970 at Gävle. Many fascinating locos and coaches were saved by both museums, in some cases well over 100 years ago, and long before preservation became a reality in many other countries.

I have been privileged to visit several delightful railways in both countries; two charming former industrial 600mm Swedish railways I have missed are the Ohsbanen in Småland and the Böda Skogsjärnväg in the far north of Öland, the long, narrow island off the country's south east coast. They are both somewhat remote but I hope to visit them one day!

Rune Bergstedt, John Browning, Stig Gustavsson, Robert Herpai, Karl-Gunnar Karlsson, the late Kurt Möller, Anders Nordebring, Lotta Sjöberg, Staffan Sjöberg, Roar Stenersen, Frank Stenvall and Håkan Zaar have all been most helpful with information and I am especially grateful to Dag Bonnedal, a long-term volunteer at the Östra Södermanlands Järnväg, for his extensive help and for correcting my many mistakes! I have drawn freely on Mr Karlsson's books about Swedish steam locos, published by Stenvalls in Malmö, and the guide books of the Gävle and Hamar museums are exceptionally informative and models of their kind.

James Waite

There have been bishops of Skara continuously for more than 1,000 years, since the earliest days after Christianity arrived in the region, and this small cathedral city, 125km northeast of Gothenburg, is the home of the oldest diocese in Sweden. It became the hub of the Västergötland-Göteborgs Järnvägar, Sweden's largest 891mm gauge system, and was the location of its repair shops and one of its main loco depots. Discussions about a railway to connect lakes Vänern and Vättern began in 1872. The initial intention to build to the 802mm gauge was soon changed to 891mm, and although the line between Hjo, on Vättern and Stenstorp was first off the mark as the country's first successful 891mm line, the continuation from Stenstorp through Skara to Lidköping, on Vänern soon followed, being opened by King Oskar II on 19th November 1874. It was operated by a different company and in 1915 became a part of VGJ. The city eventually became a junction from which several routes radiated, including a direct main line to Gothenburg which was completed in 1900. At their greatest extent VGJ and its associated railways had a route network of over 400km. VGJ was nationalised and became a part of SJ in 1948. In the 1960s and 1970s some of its lines were converted to standard gauge but most of the system was closed. There were no passenger services after August 1970 and the last freight train ran in 1987. Here VGJ 2-6-0T no 4 (Motala 193/1898) emerges from the roundhouse at Skara on 17 July 2007. The large depot and shops complex now serves the Skara-Lundsbrunns Järnvägar, which runs northwards from the city and is one of two sections of VGJ which operate as heritage railways.

No 4 stands on the turntable at Skara on 17 July 2007. The preservation society here had its origins in a decision by the local authority in 1965 to save one of VGJ's old engines as a reminder of the important role that the railway used to play in the life of the city. They looked around for volunteer support and when this was forthcoming purchased VGJ 2-8-0 no 29 in 1967. By 1971 the volunteers had restored the loco to working order and she saw occasional use on special trains until freight traffic on the last surviving railway through the city ceased in 1984. In the same year the Skara-Lundsbrunn line, along with the roundhouse, shops and part of the extensive station at Skara, were made available to the society. No 29 was regarded as being a serviceable loco when I first visited in 2007 although she was in the shops for overhaul. More recently she has been offsite for a major refurbishment. In her absence trains were worked by no 4, but since 2020 she has also been out of service and currently services are worked by SJ 2-6-2T no 3037 which is on loan from the Wadstena-Folgesta Järnväg in Småland, not a VGJ loco though a very welcome visitor. The railway acquired no 4 in 1994 after she had spent many years preserved on the quayside at Hjo as a memorial to the old Hjo-Stenstorp Järnväg, which never became part of VGJ and remained independent until it was nationalised along with VGJ in 1948. At least some of HGJ's locos carried polished brass domes throughout its independent existence and looked very smart, but sadly none have survived.

No 4 is well into her journey from Skara to Lundsbrunn on 17 July 2007 and has passed Myråsen, the summit of the line and the second highest point anywhere on the old VGJ system. After the SJ takeover No 4 underwent substantial reconstruction at the Kalmar loco factory in 1950, emerging with a new, winter-friendly cab and a high-pitched superheated boiler. Her appearance was radically altered and many people believe it would be more appropriate for her to carry her SJ livery as S5p class no 3094. The leading coach is one of three teak-clad vehicles on the line which were built for the Stockholm-Roslagens Järnväg by ASEA between 1936 and 1939. With its busy suburban traffic SRJ was the source of many of the coaches now running on Sweden's heritage railways. The second coach was an island-dweller! It was built by Fole in Visby, the capital of the island of Gotland out in the Baltic Sea between the Swedish mainland and Latvia, and ran in Öland, and the third one is another former Öland vehicle. Out on the station forecourt at Lundsbrunn is Rydénska Huset, once a general store which has been in the ownership of the Rydén family since 1910. It now houses Sigfrid and Folke's Café, run by two sisters who serve amazing home-made produce. I'm tempted to say that their smörgåsbord must be among the best in Sweden, but travellers on the country's heritage railways will soon find that high-quality food served in enjoyable surroundings is seldom far away!

2-8-0 no 29 (Motala 836/1937), and her sister no 30, were the most modern 2-8-0s to work for VGJ. No 29 moved away from the Västergötland system under SJ and ended up in store in sidings at Verkebäck harbour near Västervik, on Sweden's east coast, which today is served by another fine heritage railway (see page 36). She became SJ Gp class no 3118. While undergoing overhaul at Borås works in 1954 she was fitted with the boiler from VGJ no 21. Although this loco was older she was generally similar and no 29's appearance was little changed. Here she is under repair at Skara on 17 July 2007.

The Skara railway is also home to 891mm gauge 0-6-0T STEN STURE (Fletcher Jennings 119/1873). She began life as one of two similar 0-6-0STs supplied to the Ulricehamns Järnväg, which ran to the south of Skara but was never connected to the VGJ system. In 1907 she was sold to the Stenåsen limeworks at Dala, on the Stenstorp-Hjo line, where in 1927 she was rebuilt as a side tank. Three years later she swapped her industrial existence for service on the nearby Falköping-Uddagårdans Järnväg. She only just scraped through a boiler inspection in 1949 but managed to carry on in service for a further five years, after which she was preserved first at Hällabrottet, near Örebro, between 1956 and 1982, and after that at Skara. She is one of only nine Fletcher Jennings locos to have survived anywhere in the world. Two of the others are the Talyllyn Railway's original locos, three worked at the Betchworth limestone quarry in Surrey and three are far away in Mauritius, where they once worked in its sugar industry, though the future of two of these needs to be clarified since the sugar factory where they were looked after closed a few years ago, and they are no longer on site. The Skara group began restoring STEN STURE to working order many years ago and have recommissioned her boiler, but the work is stalled while they raise funds for new wheel tyres. Here are some of her components at the Skara shops on 4 August 2015. The wheels will look familiar to those who maintain the Talyllyn and Betchworth locos! The Sten Sture name is that of two widely-respected Swedish statesmen who lived in the 1400s and 1500s.

SJ no 3042 (Falun 503/1943) was one of three Gp class 2-8-0s. They were updated versions of VGJ nos 29 and 30 and were built for service on the 891mm gauge lines which SJ had recently taken over in Småland. On 17 July 2008 she was on display at the back of the museum building at the Anten-Gräfsnäs Järnväg, the other section of the old VGJ system which now operates as a heritage railway, though she has since moved to the Västervik-Hultsfred line in Småland. Later in the 1940s VGJ ordered four more 2-8-0s from Motala which were almost identical save that their driving wheel diameter was 1,100mm instead of the 1,040mm on the 1943 locos. They were delivered in 1950, by which time VGJ had become part of SJ; three of them moved on to join their older sisters in Småland after SJ's 891mm gauge services in Västergötland were dieselised in 1954. One of them was also saved and is awaiting restoration at the Uppsala-Länna Järnväg. Motala built another five with a higher degree of superheat for SJ's 3ft 6ins gauge system in 1948 and 1949 but its days were already numbered and they were designed with conversion to the narrower gauge in mind, with minimal work. In the event this never happened and all five were scrapped in 1966 and 1967. The 1948-50 locos on both gauges carried Witte-type smoke deflectors and looked most impressive.

The Anten line is a part of the VGJ extension to Gothenburg which opened in 1900. Unlike the Skara railway there was no workshop or engine shed for the preservationists to take over but they have constructed a most attractive building which houses both a running shed and this neat and well-equipped repair and restoration facility. On 17 July 2007 the Ruda-Oskarshamns Järnväg's 2-6-0T no 3 (951/1910), later SJ S9p class no 3026, was undergoing heavy overhaul. ROJ merged with a connecting line to become the Östra Smålands Järnväg, which was the southernmost part of the Östergötland and Småland system and connected Växjö with Oskarshamn, a major port on Sweden's Baltic coast. SJ's Tp class 2-6-2 diesels replaced steam on many of its 891mm gauge lines during the 1950s but they were too heavy for ÖSJ and its freight trains continued to be steam-worked until 1963, latterly by the Gp class 2-8-0s. By then it was SJ's last steam-worked 891mm line. No 3026 was withdrawn in 1965 and three years later was acquired by what was initially known as the Stora Lundby Järnvägsmuseum, which had been set up by enthusiasts in 1965 to run museum trains on the Sjövik-Gråbo section of VGJ near Gothenburg. It closed in 1967, along with the line on to Gothenburg to enable a part to be converted to a suburban light railway, and when the line north from Sjövik through Anten as far as Nossebro closed in 1970 they switched their focus to saving the Anten-Gräfsnäs section. No 3026 hauled its first heritage train in the following year.

On 4 August 2015 ROJ no 3's place in the workshops at Anten had been taken by the Byvalla-Långshyttans Järnväg's 2-8-0T no 6 (Motala 566/1916). BLJ was a 27km-long 891mm-gauge railway to the west of Gävle which was built as an industrial line in 1891 to serve the local ironworks (see page 90). After pressure from the local communities it introduced public passenger and goods services in 1893, but its approach seems to have been somewhat begrudging. It never provided continuous brakes and, despite continuing to operate until 1964, always relied solely on steam traction and never sullied itself with a diesel! No 6 moved to Gothenburg in June 1965 on hire to the Stora Lundby Järnvägsmuseum. Later that year they purchased her as their first loco, established themselves at VGJ's Gothenburg engine shed and fitted her up with air brakes. On the left is the boiler of VGJ 4-6-0 no 31 (Henschel 25935/1941), later SJ B4p class no 3110, with its pointy smokebox door. She has been undergoing restoration to working order for many years.

No 31 was delivered from Henschel's factory in Kassel to Sweden via Denmark, with only a short sea crossing. It may seem surprising that a relatively insignificant Swedish railway could obtain this one-off loco at a time when Germany's industrial facilities were operating on a war footing. The explanation was probably that large quantities of iron ore from northern Sweden were vital to the German war effort, so much so that the accumulated wealth which they generated made a considerable contribution to Sweden's postwar prosperity and the generous funding for its welfare state, at least until it enjoyed new income streams after joining the EU. The Germans may well have judged it to be worthwhile accommodating orders from the country, and anyway the foreign exchange which they brought was probably very welcome. At one point VGJ considered the purchase of two locos to handle increasing traffic during the war, and there has been speculation that two may have been built and that one was lost at sea, though there is no real evidence to support this. At the end of her SJ life she arrived at Gothenburg engine shed in 1965 en route from the Skara store to SJ's scrapyard at Vislanda, in Småland, just as the Stora Lundby Järnvägsmuseum was becoming established there. At first the museum society did not intend to preserve her but several active volunteers successfully raised funds and bought her in the following year. On 4 August 2015 her chassis and some of her wheels were standing in another part of the workshops at Anten. She was fitted with Witte smoke deflectors and a streamlined cab front as well as that pointy smokebox door, which all made for a very imposing machine.

I have visited Anten five times since 2007 and on each occasion the operating loco has been a much older VGJ 4-6-0, no 24 (Nohab 982/1911), one of a pair built as express locos in that year. A third one followed in 1915. VGJ's express trains had previously been worked by four 4-4-0s, nos 5-8 built in 1899, the design of which was based on a series of 4-4-0Ts built around the same time for the 3ft 6ins gauge lines in south eastern Sweden. The 4-4-0s were all scrapped after the diesels arrived in 1954, along with nearly all the other 891mm gauge steam locos in Västergötland, though one of the 3ft 6ins 4-4-0Ts has survived (see page 27). I have always thought that no 24 is a very pretty machine indeed. She was bought by the Stora Lundby Järnvägsmuseum in 1965 as their second loco. On 14 July 2009 she has admirers as she prepares to set off from Anten station. The leading van was built by Vetlanda Mekaniska Verkstad in 1907.

No 24 stands in the yard at Anten on 14 July 2009. She looks every inch the high-stepping loco which she is, designed for a maximum speed of 70kph, very fast for the Swedish narrow gauge, though the speed limit on VGJ was never that high. She became SJ B2p class 3105.

On 17 July 2008 no 24 runs through a cutting at Humlebo, close to the southern end of Lake Anten. The leading vehicle is one of two 4-wheeled coaches on AGJ which were built in 1911 by Kalmar Verkstad for the Kalmar-Torsås Järnväg. The second coach, a delightful 4-wheeled vehicle with its clerestory, was built in 1905 by Fole at Visby for the Lidköping-Skara-Stenstorps Järnväg, the 1874 railway which became a part of VGJ in 1915. AGJ runs close to the lake for much of its length and was chosen for preservation partly on account of its attractive scenery. Like most of Sweden's heritage railways it has a short operating season, which usually starts in June and continues only until mid-August.

Gräfsnäs is the northern terminus of the Anten line. Just to the south of the town a castle, or slott in Swedish, overlooks the northern end of the lake. It was built in about 1550 and became derelict after being ravaged by fire in 1834. Even before the 1900 railway was built the ruins and the 28-acre park around them were a popular tourist attraction, and in 1911 the railway company bought it and built a halt, called Gräfsnäs Slottsparken, to accommodate the ever-growing crowds of visitors who were attracted there. Gräfsnäs remains a much-visited place, not only for the park but also for the beautiful lakeside beaches close by, and this was another reason why this section of VGJ was chosen for the heritage operation. On 17 July 2008 no 24 approaches the site of the Slottsparken halt with a southbound train. The leading coach was built by the Hessleholm carriage factory in Skåne in 1904 for the Karlstad-Munkfors Järnväg, later a constituent of the Nordmark-Klarälvens Järnväg which was never nationalised and, other than SRJ, had become Sweden's only narrow gauge railway offering a public service by the time it closed in 1990 (see pages 85-89). The second coach is one of twenty four which were built by the Bautzen factory in Germany for SRJ between 1920 and 1944, five of which are now at AGJ. The earlier ones were originally fitted with open end platforms, though many were later closed in. This coach, SRJ no 97, was built in 1939 and is the only one of the five to remain as built in this respect.

No 24 passes Humlebo with a southbound train on 14 July 2009. The lake is just visible between the trees to the right. Nos 4, 24, 29 and 31 were amongst a few of the old VGJ steam locos which were transferred to a strategic reserve at Skara roundhouse when most of the others were scrapped after the dieselisation in 1954. The idea was that they would be available for use in case of war or other emergency, and had the reserve not been created probably none of them would have survived. No 4 moved to Hjo for preservation in 1962 and the others were dispersed in 1965, happily just as the Stora Lundby Järnvägsmuseum was being established. The leading 4-wheeled coach was built by Vabis at Södertälje in 1910 for the Växjö-Virserums Järnväg in Småland, which later became part of the Växjö-Åseda-Hultsfreds Järnväg. Behind it is SRJ no 97. Vabis was founded in 1891 by Surahammars Bruk (see page 53) to build railway carriages. It branched out into automobile manufacture in 1897 and today is the huge Scania truck-building business, still based in Södertälje.

No 24 heads through the fields close to the lake near Humlebo with a northbound train on 14 July 2009. In addition to the three Nohab-built 4-6-0s two generally similar ones were supplied to VGJ by Henschel in 1922, while Nohab built another one in 1915 for the Kalmar-Berga Järnväg. All these locos, along with no 31, the loco built by Henschel in 1941, were fitted with 1,300mm diameter driving wheels, the largest ever used on the 891mm gauge. Swedish railways bought many locos from German builders in the years after the First World War, as the prices they were charging during their country's post-war economic malaise were significantly lower than Swedish manufacturers could offer. The second vehicle, with the ribbed sides characteristic of Swedish steel coaches, dates from 1941. It is one of three with all-welded bodies which were built by Svenska Maskinverken, one for VGJ and two for SRJ. This one is SRJ no 104. The next coach, only partially visible, was built by Atlas of Stockholm in 1898 for the Vikbolandsbanan, a part of the Östergötland network.

On 17 July 2008 no 24 passes a level crossing immediately outside Gräfsnäs station with a southbound train. In VGJ's early years trains made an extended stop at Gräfsnäs for passengers to buy refreshments, and a separate café was built but, unlike the main station building, it has not survived.

A final view of no 24 as she approaches Anten on 17 July 2008. She is about to pass a storage building and sidings some distance north of the station, needed so that all the ten locos which the society has accumulated since 1965 can be kept under cover, as well as providing yard space for numerous items of rolling stock.

The huge Nohab loco-building factory in Trollhättan was once the largest anywhere in Sweden but fell silent after the company became insolvent in 1979. A part is now occupied by the Innovatum museum and one of the exhibits is 2-4-0T TROLLHÄTTAN (Nohab 1/1865), the factory's very first loco. I saw her there on 4 August 2015. She was built for the Uddevala-Vänersborg-Herrjunga Järnväg as a more or less direct copy of two locos built for the Boräs-Herrljunga Järnväg two years earlier by Slaughter, Gruning & Co in Bristol, the predecessors of the Avonside Engine Co. UVHJ and BHJ were two of Sweden's four 4ft railways, all of them built before the widespread adoption of the 891mm gauge. UVHJ was converted to standard gauge in 1899. TROLLHÄTTAN was withdrawn but was put on show at the Nohab factory on account of her pioneering role in its history. She moved to Järnvägmuseet in 1918 and is now on loan to Innovatum.

Delary, in southwestern Småland, was home to an ironworks which changed to producing paper pulp in the 1870s. In 1875 it built a short railway with a gauge of 643mm or 26 Swedish inches, initially to bring in peat as fuel. The line was gradually extended to Strömsnäsbruk, 16km away, and used to collect logs floated on the River Lagan. In 1897 the standard gauge Skåne-Smålands Järnväg reached Strömsnäsbruk, crossing the narrow gauge near the river. At about the same time another paper factory was built there, and in later years pulp was transported from Delary for it to process. The Delary plant had clearly not lost all its old ironworking skills because between 1878 and 1916 it built four locos for the railway - and what unusual machines they were! The first was a 2-2-0T, but it lasted only from 1878 until 1890. The others were 0-8-0T's, numbered 1 - 3 and built over a period of thirty three years. Nos 1 EDWARD ENGESTRÖM (Delary 2/1884) and 2 RUDOLF THOMSON (Delary 3/1887) started out with small saddle tanks but were fitted with larger side ones after the line reached Strömsnäsbruk. Their first three axles were positioned very close together at the front. There was a long gap under the firebox and the fourth axle was underneath the distinctly roomy cab. Fitting in the two drive cranks for the inside cylinders and the four eccentrics for the valve gear between the inside frames of a loco with such a narrow gauge must have involved considerable ingenuity! EDWARD ENGESTRÖM now resides at Delary, close to the old factory, and on 4 August 2015 she was enjoying the last of the late evening sunshine. The line possessed a fleet of modern and sturdy 2-axle wagons, many of which now see service on the preserved Östra Sodermanlands Järnväg.

No 3 AUG. SCHMITZ (Delary 4/1916) and her little coach are preserved in the station yard at Strömsnäsbruk, and in this view on 4 August 2015 the loco's unusual wheel arrangement can be clearly seen. She and EDWARD ENGESTRÖM now live under wide-roofed shelters which cast shadows for much of a sunny day, and are best visited when the sun is low. I thought it was well worth making the long journey to visit these most interesting machines, so much so that the management once issued an instruction that they should be restricted to about 35kph; by comparison the limit on the 600mm lines was 20 or 25kph. There was little traffic on the wide country road which connects Strömsnäsbruk and Delary, and I was able to photograph them both at sunset, thanks to the long northern dusk and some spirited driving! The 0-8-0Ts were reputed to be fast and free-steaming machines, so much so that the management once issued an instruction that they should be restricted to about 35kph; by comparison the limit on the 600mm lines was 20 or 25kph. RUDOLF THOMSON was damaged in an engine shed fire in 1928 and was rebuilt as a fireless loco. There were also no 4 MAX ENGESTRÖM (Sentinel 7543/1928) and a O&K 0-4-0T named KAROLINA, which came secondhand in 1946. The line closed in 1959. By then the steam locos had been withdrawn, though internal traffic, worked by two Simplex diesels, continued at the factories until 1974. They closed in 1981. Today KAROLINA runs on the Böda Skogsjärnväg while one Simplex is on the heritage Munkedals Järnväg, both converted to 600mm gauge. Sadly the Sentinel and the fireless loco were scrapped. The standard gauge railway closed to passengers in 1968 and to freight between 1963 and 2000. Now the section through Strömsnäsbruk has become the Skåne-Smålands Järnvägsföreningen, a heritage railway which is mostly devoted to the SSJ but it has also taken AUG. SCHMITZ under its wing. There's a seven-road standard gauge roundhouse at Strömsnäsbruk station and an extension at its southern end with 643mm gauge track which perhaps once housed AUG. SCHMITZ and her friends.

Nowadays the small town of Limhamn has become a suburb to the south west of Malmö and is the place where the long Øresund bridge across to Denmark begins. The town's name means "lime harbour", and for many years its prosperity came from two abundant commodities, limestone and herrings. The limestone quarry extended over one square kilometre and is said to be the biggest hole in the ground in northern Europe. A 891mm gauge railway was built in 1871 to carry the stone through the streets of the town to a cement factory on the coast. It was worked by horses until the first steam locos arrived in 1884, and was electrified in 1949. The line was replaced by underground conveyor belts in 1967 and the quarry closed in the 1990s. It possessed no fewer than twenty one steam locos, all 0-4-0Ts, three of which have been preserved. Most of them were scrapped in the early 1950s, though the two youngest ones remained in stock for another ten years. No 13 (Krauss Munich 6051/1908) has been an exhibit at the Malmö Tekniska Museum since 1960 where I saw her on 5 August 2015. No 15 was sold in 1965 to Kaabs AB which ran a scrap metal business in Ängelholm, and was plinthed there until 1994 when she moved to Bornholm, the Danish island off Sweden's south coast. No 16 has also become an island-dweller and is in store at the Gotlands Hesselby Järnväg (see pages 40-49).

0-4-0WT no 3 of the Höganäs colliery railway (Krauss Munich 1320/1883) is a much smaller loco than her Munich-built sister from the Limhamn railway. Höganäs is a small town on the coast of the Kullaberg peninsula north of Helsingborg, and was the site of a colliery, which opened in 1797, and also clay pits. In the following year a railway, generally considered to be the first in Sweden, opened to transport the coal to the harbour. The original rails were made of wood and were replaced by iron ones in 1827. It is believed to have been 1,332mm gauge at first but in 1874 it was rebuilt as a conventional 760mm gauge system and steam operation was introduced. At its greatest extent it was about 43km long and altogether no fewer that thirteen locos operated there, built between 1874 and 1930. In later years, at least, considerable quantities of clay were transported and probably also other materials as factories serving a diverse range of manufacturing industries were established. The last collieries had gone over to producing clay by the time they closed in the 1960s. The town is still well known throughout Sweden for Höganäs Keramik, a huge ceramics factory served by the clay pits. No 3 is one of two surviving locos. She was withdrawn in 1957 and became an exhibit at the Höganäs museum where she stayed for forty years before moving to the Frövi Maskin- and Bruksbanemuseum, much further north in Örebro county. Here she stands at its entrance on 22 September 2015.

0-4-0WT no 9 (Ljunggrens 31/1917) is the other surviving Höganäs loco. She was also withdrawn in 1957 and put on display at Kaabs's scrap yard in Ängelholm until she was moved away in 1964 and shortly afterwards replaced by Limhamn no 15. Her new home was the regional museum in Kristianstad, the town in which Ljunggrens was based. The firm was founded in 1861 and closed in 1925, but part of its impressive factory complex still exists and has been converted into apartments. In 1979 she was transferred to Järnvägmuseet Kristianstad, the town's newly-established railway museum. She is now kept in their storage building, just along the road from the old Ljunggrens factory. It is not normally accessible to the public but the staff helpfully opened it up for me on 18 July 2017 and pulled back the loco's protective tarpaulin so far as they could for me to photograph her.

The Kristianstad museum includes a 600mm gauge railway. It threads its way through the standard gauge sidings out in the museum yard and involves a mixed gauge section over the turntable which gives access to them, which must make for an unusual ride! It is worked by this pretty little 0-4-0T, built in 1980 by Christer and Arne Bengtsson at Glimåkra as their no 1. Her coach looks as though it is also recently-built but I have not found out any of its history. Unfortunately my visit on 18 July 2017 did not coincide with an operating day and the little train was standing at the line's platform inside the main museum building.

Kristianstad was one of the principal towns served by the 3ft 6ins system in south eastern Sweden. Interesting though the Ljunggrens and the Bengtssons' locos were and the old Ljunggrens buildings, my main reason for visiting the town was to see SJ's 3ft 6ins gauge 4-4-0T no 4006 (Nohab 625/1901), originally no 19 BODEKULL of the Vastra Blekinge Järnväg. This attractive loco is one of the series of 4-4-0Ts on which the VGJ 4-4-0s were based. She was withdrawn in 1959 and has been preserved at Kristianstad since 1965, now as another resident at the museum store. Only two of Sweden's 3ft 6ins gauge steam locos have survived. She is normally hemmed in by other stock, but the museum staff very kindly drew her out into the daylight for me on 18 July 2017, a difficult process which required the services of an enormous farm tractor. They told me it was the first time she had ventured out for several years and they seemed to enjoy the occasion as much as I did.

SJ 2-6-0 no 4013 (Nohab 836/1907) is the other surviving 3ft 6ins steam loco. She was built for the Blekinge Kustbanor, a system which grew to a length of 252km after taking over several smaller railways. No 4013 was withdrawn in 1965 but found a new home at Järnvägmuseet. Here she stands in a storage building, one of two old roundhouses at their principal site in the southern outskirts of Gävle, on 14 July 2016. It's a shame that neither of these very pretty 3ft 6ins locos is on public display in view of the significant role that the gauge played in Sweden's railway history. SJ began to set aside historic material for preservation as long ago as 1906. For many years after the museum moved to Gävle in 1970 its principal display was housed in the adjoining roundhouse. It was only possible to show a small part of its extensive collection there, and in recent years the public has sometimes been admitted to its large storage building and restoration shop known as Tåghallen at Nynäs, in the north west of the city, and a train service between the two sites has been provided. In 2018 the museum closed for extensive reconstruction. It was initially scheduled to reopen in 2020, but the project has been delayed by the Covid pandemic and as I write this the reopening of both it and Tåghallen is scheduled for the summer of 2023. Maybe space will be found to display no 4013.

Västervik is a port town on the east coast of Sweden about 220kms south of Stockholm. The 891mm gauge Hultsfred-Västervik Järnväg is 68kms long and opened in 1879. At Hultsfred it made an end-on connection with the Växjö-Åseda-Hultsfreds Järnväg, which continued for another 117km to Växjö. With the 3ft 6ins gauge line which came up from the south as well as a standard gauge main line, Växjö was one of the world's few towns which was served by trains of three different gauges. The section out from Västervik as far as a junction at Jenny was shared with the 891mm gauge Västervik-Åtvidaberg-Bersbo Järnväg, which opened the previous year, and the name of which was always officially abbreviated to "WÅB" after the old spelling of "Wästervik" and without a "J" at the end. HVJ and WÅB, along with the Norsholm-Bersbo Järnväg further north, merged in 1924 to form the Norsholm-Västervik-Hultsfred Järnväg which was nationalised in 1949. The Västervik to Jenny section became mixed gauge in 1964 when the line north from Västervik was converted to standard gauge. Now the whole of HVJ is a flourishing heritage railway. On 11 July 2015 SJ L18p class 2-6-0 no 3147 (Nohab 848/1907) was waiting at Verkebäck station before continuing her journey to Ankarsrum. She was built as VHJ no 22 and has spent her entire life on the line.

For many years 891mm gauge trains ran through from Västervik to Växjö over the old Växjö-Åseda-Hultsfreds Järnväg which had been involved in various mergers of its own until it was nationalised in 1941. The 187km journey must have ranked as one of Europe's longer narrow gauge rides. Passenger traffic ended in 1984, in the face of determined opposition by many throughout the country who valued the access to the Småland countryside which it provided. By then it was SJ's last narrow gauge line offering a passenger service. It was bought for preservation but various difficulties arose and eventually a considerable length at the Växjö end was abandoned completely. The present heritage operation between Västervik and Hultsfred was established in 2003. Trains run daily over the whole route between early July and mid-August and on some days in June and September, usually worked by former SJ railcars. When my wife and I visited in 2015 the line also saw steam trains running over the 24km section between Västervik and Ankarsrum during four weekends in July and August, but since then the steam locos have been out of action for some years in need of overhaul. Much of the railway runs through forest but here no 3147 (Nohab 848/1907) was making her way through a more open stretch midway between Fårhult and Ankarsrum on 11 July 2015.

No 3147 has run round her train at Ankarsrum on 11 July 2015 and has been waiting for the railcar set seen in this photo to pass before beginning her return journey to Västervik. Seventy two passenger railcars were built for SJ between 1952 and 1958 at a factory in Umeå owned by Hilding Carlsson, who had started building railbuses in 1917 and whose business came to dominate the Swedish railcar market in the 1930s and 1940s. They were initially classified YBo5p, and became class YP under a computer-friendly scheme introduced in 1970. There were also seventy three trailers and four freight-only cars. They worked on all SJ's 891mm gauge lines on the Swedish mainland, though not on the railways of Öland or Gotland. Västervik received some of the first batch to be built and SJ withdrew the last ones in 1984 when their service on the Västervik-Växjö line ended. Twenty railcars and ten trailers have been preserved and they play an important role on several of Sweden's heritage railways. The first ones were painted cream and green, but when the Y6 standard gauge version appeared in 1953 carrying this orange and cream livery it was also was adopted on the narrow gauge. The cars of both gauges with the striking colour scheme became much loved, not just by railway enthusiasts but amongst a much wider section of the Swedish public because of the access to the countryside which they represented. There were no fewer than 378 of the standard gauge Y6s and the Y7s which were developed from them, and 321 trailers, though none were built by Hilding Carlsson. The last standard gauge cars were withdrawn from regular passenger service in 1989, but they still work the Gävle-Nynäs museum operation when Tåghallen is open. Many have been preserved throughout Scandinavia, and one operates on the Nene Valley Railway near Peterborough.

A period scene at Ankarsrum's attractive station on 11 July 2015 complete with no 3147, just visible behind the building, and a Volvo 121 on the forecourt. Still often seen in Sweden, these much-loved classic cars were built for ten years from 1957. The Aktiveum industrial museum occupies what was once Ankarsrum Bruk, an ironworks close to the station. Sweden's early ironworks were small-scale affairs and some of them lasted long enough to be served by railways of several gauges and, more recently, to be preserved as industrial monuments. We have already met the one at Delary and will meet more later in this book.

The lady fireman sets the points as no 3147 runs round her train at Västervik on 11 July 2015, with the town's fine station building as a backdrop. Sweden's older stations are often large and ornate structures, and the one at Västervik is exceptionally striking. Until very recently Västervik was more of a commercial port than a seaside holiday town, but such is the demand for accommodation from visitors to the countryside of eastern Småland that hotel space was at a premium when my wife and I looked for somewhere to stay in the town. We needed to search further afield, but this turned out to be a real blessing as we found Tofvehult, a guesthouse about 24km away at a quiet and peaceful spot out in the countryside near Västrum, on the spit of land which separates lakes Toven and Ålsjön. It was truly delightful place which was once a family home for Lena Göransson, a former international model who now writes cookery books as well as running the guesthouse with her husband Peter. Tofvehult provided just the right combination of comfort and informality - and Lena's food was out of this world!

HVJ's locos are kept in a fine 9-bay roundhouse at Västervik, the largest on any of the country's preserved 891mm gauge lines. SJ 2-6-2T no 3037 (Kalmar 1/1919) began life as no 15 of the Kalmar-Torsås Järnväg. She was withdrawn in 1963 and after a period on display at Kalmar moved to the Wadstena-Fogelsta Järnväg in 1984. More recently she was on loan to HVJ and on 11 July 2015 was under repair in the roundhouse at Västervik. In 2022 she moved to the Skara-Lundsbrunn line. The backlighting on her numberplate shows an unusual feature of the plates attached to SJ's less important locos, which were made of cast iron. While their lettering was cast onto the rim the number was only painted on, whereas the plates on their top-flight machines were made of polished brass with raised numerals. HVJ is also home to 2-8-0T no 3050, built by Motala in 1920 for the railway serving Öland, which is on loan from Järnvägmuseet, and 2-8-0 no 3042 (see page 9). Both need major restoration, but there's no prospect that this will be carried out in the near future, and also no word of when no 3147 will return to service. Björn Ulvaeus, of ABBA fame, spent much of his childhood in Västervik, and to give something back has embarked upon a mission to make the district more tourist-friendly. His hotel Slottsholmen, with some spectacular architecture and equally amazing views, opened in 2018 on a headland overlooking Västervik harbour, and is now run by his daughter Anna. Maybe he could be encouraged to extend his benevolence to the town by helping the return of steam to HVJ!

No 3147 runs alongside Verkebäcksviken, the Verkebäck estuary, in the early evening of 11 July 2015. Malorca, the boat at the quay in the foreground, was built in 1944 at Gamleby, just a short distance away. She had once been a fishing boat but later was registered as a recreational craft based at Bohus-Björkö, an island off the coast of Västergötland near Gothenburg. I was told that she had recently changed hands and had moved to Verkebäck to be converted to a houseboat. The quay and harbour were once served by a branch line about 650m long from Verkebäck station. While Ankarsrum Bruk was functioning its products travelled there by rail for onward transport by sea, and it was here many years later that some of SJ's narrow gauge steam locos were stored after their working days were over.

The Hvetlanda-Sävsjö Järnvägar, later part of the Vetlanda Järnvägar, lay inland from the Västervik system. Its 0-6-0T no 4 A WILH PETRI (Motala 239/1900) has been a non-working exhibit at the Anten line's museum since she arrived on loan from Järnvägmuseet. I saw her there on 4 August 2015. Her name refers to Wilhelm Petri who was a director of the bank which financed the line. At some stage of her career she was rebuilt for one-man operation to enable the fireman to act also as guard. VJ was taken over by SJ in 1945 and no 4 became Kp class no 3048. Her elder sister no 3 (Motala 107/1889), an identical loco and another STEN STURE, left the comparative warmth of Småland earlier in 1945 to move to the Ny Ålesund colliery railway in far-away Svalbard (see page 119), but perhaps didn't enjoy life there as she was scrapped only three years later. Outside cylinder 0-6-0Ts like these became very much a standard type on Sweden's 891mm gauge railways during the late 1800s and early 1900s. Motala built seventeen between 1884 and 1905 and Kristinehamn sixteen between 1883 and 1901, while Munktells, Helsingborg and Falun produced just one each, in 1886, 1901 and 1902. Ljunggrens built two much larger ones for a timber railway at Vallvik, one in 1909 and another in 1914. Nohab built twelve between 1875 and 1890, plus one more in 1909 and the very last of the type, another loco for Vallvik, in 1928. This photo introduces us to the turbine spark-arrester at the base of the chimney, one of the distinctive features of many Swedish locomotives.

2,573 Brigadelok 0-8-0Ts had been ordered for the German army by the time the First World War ended. Many of those which survived into peacetime were seized as booty by the victorious powers, and others were soon put up for sale very cheaply. Twelve found their way to Sweden, including nine built in 1919 which must have been virtually brand new, and three have been preserved. This loco, Borsig 10474/1919, was the army's no 2702. She started her Swedish life as no 3 at Aspa Bruk, a pulp and saw mill at the northern end of Vättern, whose 600mm gauge forestry line later became home to several pieces of equipment from the public lines after they closed, thanks to which they survived into the preservation era. She acquired the nickname GRÅLLAN, or Grey Mare, perhaps because the Brigadeloks arrived in Sweden painted in the German Army's grey livery. In 1948 she moved to a cellulose factory at Eds Bruk, a little to the north of Västervik and 4km inland from the Baltic coast at Helgenäs, which replaced a small ironworks there after it closed in 1899. The factory's product was used in paper manufacture. A 600mm gauge railway to Helgenäs opened in 1889, back in its ironworks days, and GRÅLLAN became its no 3. She was withdrawn in the 1950s and found a new home at the Östergötlands Järnvägsmuseum in Linköping which had been founded two years earlier. I saw her there on 12 July 2017. Eds Bruk's no 1 HELGENÄS, a tiny and very pretty 0-4-2ST (Hudswell Clarke 346/1889) was withdrawn in 1937. She has also been preserved, initially at Eds Bruk until moving to the enthusiast-run Östra Sodermanlands Järnväg in 1965 (see page 74). The cellulose factory closed in 1992 and the premises remained vacant for nearly thirty years until part became an art gallery in 2020.

The Norra Östergötlands Jarnvag was formed in 1896 from an amalgamation of several local railways which served the northern part of Östergötland. By 1906 it was offering services between Norrköping and Örebro, and began to buy much larger locos to befit its status as a regional main line. NÖJ's 2-8-2Ts nos 17 and 18 (Motala 667 and 668/1920) were much bigger than their predecessors. It did not acquire any more for many years until a third 2-8-2T, built to a slightly updated design, arrived in 1946. The railway was taken over by SJ in 1950, when the three locos became their class N4p and were numbered 3059-61. They were all withdrawn in 1963 and no 18 became an exhibit at the Linköping museum in 1967, one year after the railway closed. Two of NÖJ's earlier locos, 2-6-0T HADDEBO (Nohab 56/1875) and 2-4-0T ROXEN (Nohab 197/1885) migrated to Ny Ålesund in 1919, but were probably scrapped before VJ's STEN STURE arrived there. Both the steam locos at Linköping were presented to Järnvägsmuseum some years ago, bringing the number of narrow gauge steam locos it owns to ten, but only the Frykstad loco had actually been displayed in Gävle before the recent closure for rebuilding (see page 84).

Island railways often have a distinctive character and those on Gotland were no exception. Hesselby station lay on the Slite-Roma Järnväg, which served the eastern part of the island, and is now the headquarters of the 891mm gauge Gotlands Hesselby Järnväg, an excellent heritage railway. On 26 July 2017 SIRJ's 2-8-0T no 3 DALHEM (Henschel 18152/1920) stood at the station before the start of the day's services. Gotland was once served by no fewer than six railway companies, but closures and mergers had reduced them to three by the time its railways were nationalised in 1947. At first they were consolidated into Gotlands Järnvägar, the oldest and longest line on the island. The following year the railways all became part of SJ, but none of them fared well. Only occasional services ran on SIRJ after 1953 and it was abandoned two years later.

The northern end of Hesselby station is little changed from SIRJ days, and the large modern buildings where the heritage stock is kept and the locos are serviced are to the south. Goods wagons stand outside the old goods shed on the right which, like the main station building, dates back to the railway's opening in 1902. The distinctive structure on the left was built in 1939 by Gotländska Lantmännens Centralförening, or the Gotland Farmers' Co-operative, as a store for its members' produce. It now houses a small museum devoted to Gotland's railways. Hesselby was the largest intermediate station on the old line, but is actually located in Dalhem, a large village after which the loco has been named ever since she was built. The Hesselby name is that of a nearby farm and was chosen because Dune, the next station to the north east, also lay within the village boundaries. I had intended to arrive in good time on 26 July 2017 to see DALHEM being prepared, but became navigationally challenged and took a wrong turn. When I eventually reached the station I found that she was being used for a professional photo-shoot with lots of shunting manoeuvres around the yard before the start of public services, and this was one of them.

DALHEM stands with her train at Hesselby on 26 July 2017. She was withdrawn in 1960 when the last of the island's railways was closed, apart from a steeply graded branch between the station and the harbour at Visby which lasted for another two years. In 1963, shortly before the track was lifted, she was towed together with several wagons and one carriage from Visby to Roma station with the intention that they should form a memorial to the old railways. Roma is in the centre of the island, and was an appropriate location for their new home as the three railways which survived to be nationalised converged there, and it was the hub of the system. A sugar beet processing plant was established in the village between 1892 and 1894 and two of the three lines, including SIRJ, were built primarily to serve it. DALHEM and her train gradually deteriorated and plans were made in the early 1970s to move them to the mainland where it was thought they would be better looked after. A group of enthusiasts was spurred into action to keep them in Gotland. In February 1972 they met in Visby and formed a museum association to take care of them. At the same time the old Hesselby station was put up for sale and their aims soon expanded to include construction of a heritage railway on the old SIRJ trackbed from there to Roma. Its first section as far as Eken, a little under 1km away, reopened in 1978.

In the early 2000s GHJ embarked on a major extension, largely financed by EU grants. The 0.5km section from Eken to Munkebos opened in 2006 and it was extended for a further 1.6km via Nygård to Tule in 2013. In 2015 it was completed through to Roma, 6.5km from Hesselby. In this photo on 26 July 2017 DALHEM is midway between Nygård and Tule, running through the woods which characterise much of the revived railway, and the island scene in general. Gotland is mostly a limestone plateau, with few significant features, and the scenery in this view is typical. There is a distinctive island culture, influenced to some extent by periods of Danish and German control, though many elements are found nowhere else. Almost as many Arabic dirhams, or silver coins, have been found there as in the entire Arabic world, and ancient Roman and Greek artefacts are often uncovered. Out of a total island population of about 60,000 between 2,000 and 5,000 people speak the native Gutnish language; it derived from Old Norse, though the present-day version also draws from mainland Swedish. Many Gotlanders are fiercely proud of it, but for political reasons the Swedish government does not give it any special privileges or even recognise it, in stark contrast to the protection afforded to its five Sami tongues or, within other European countries, to languages such as Welsh, the Scottish and Irish versions of Gaelic and the indigenous tongues of Spain. UNESCO classifies it as a "definitely endangered language".

On 26 July 2017 DALHEM pauses at Tule, with its complete complement of original SIRJ buildings. There was always a passing loop here in the old days, even though it is only 3.7km from Roma. The site was purchased privately in 1982 by Märta and Ingmar Lindkvist, GHJ supporters. The station area and buildings are now owned and managed by a foundation which formally bears their name, but is usually just called Tulestiftelsen, or Tule Foundation. The main building is let out as a holiday home, and the considerable income which it generates goes towards the station's restoration and maintenance. In the old days the building's exterior was rendered with lime plaster, but it was removed soon after Tulestiftelsen took over. Gotland is very popular with tourists from the Swedish mainland, so much so that it is hard to find accommodation during the summer and charges can be sky-high – not good for the holidaymakers but very beneficial for Tule station!

DALHEM has resumed her journey after her stop at Tule and approaches Kambshagtorp on 26 July 2017. The leading van in her train also came from SIRJ. The loco became SJ no 3073 in 1947 and was the youngest of three which served SIRJ, the others being 0-6-0Ts nos 1 SLITE and 2 GUTE, both built by Kristenhamn in 1901 in readiness for its opening the following year. They were part of a batch of three which proved to be the last 891mm gauge 0-6-0Ts which the factory built, and were both scrapped in the 1950s. The third, the Ronehamn-Helmse Järnväg's no 1 RONEHAMN, was bought by the Roma factory for service on this short-lived and impoverished line, which it promoted to transport sugar beet from the south of Gotland via a junction at Helmse with GJ. RHJ ran only between 1904 and 1918, after which RONEHAMN shunted at the Roma factory until the line through the town closed in 1960. Sadly she was then scrapped. RHJ's only other piece of motive power was a second-hand steam railcar (Ljunggrens 2/1898) which was financed and owned personally by some of its directors and arrived in 1903. After 1918 it may have continued to run informally on the line until the track was lifted in 1923. It moved to another short line which ran south along the coast from Visby until it, too, closed in 1941. The railcar was scrapped soon afterwards, though its body was used as an outhouse at Visby until the 1960s. In 1891 the Kristinehamn business was leased to Karlstad Mekaniska Werkstad, often called Kamewa, which many years later became a part of the Rolls-Royce aerospace company, though this part of its business has recently reverted to Swedish control. Loco-building at Kristinehamn ended in 1902.

DALHEM and her train negotiate the final curve at the approach to Roma station. The leading coach was GJ's no 8 and was built at their workshops at Visby in 1935. The last one is a most interesting 4-wheeled coach, GJ no 43, which was built by Fole at Visby in 1898 and includes a mail sorting compartment, a kind of travelling post office! GJ operated the island's main line between Lärbro, in the north, via Visby and Roma to the southern town of Burgsvik, 117km away, which opened in stages between 1878 and 1921. Much of the extensive station yard at Roma had been redeveloped since the closure, but the northern part was undisturbed and is now the location of GHJ's new terminus. The old turntable pit is alongside the tracks and work has been carried out with a view to reinstating it. The new building originally stood at GJ's Österport station, next to one of the three gateways in the magnificent city wall at Visby which, like many of the buildings it encircles, is almost unchanged since medieval times, and is a principal reason why the city is now a UNESCO-listed world heritage site. SJ had an issue with the name of Roma station, and in 1954 renamed it Roma Kloster after a ruined twelfth-century Cistercian monastery there, supposedly to avoid confusion with the capital of Italy! 26 July 2017.

GJ's 0-6-0T no 3 GOTLAND (Nohab 89/1877] was one of three similar locos ordered for the opening of its first section, though she was exhibited at the 1878 world exhibition at Paris, where she won a silver medal. Consequently she did not reach Gotland until Spring 1879, several months after services began. She became SJ no 3063 and was bought back by Nohab after being withdrawn in 1953. They restored her to what was believed to be her original condition and in 1956 presented her to SJ to celebrate their centenary, after which she became an exhibit at Järnvägmuseet. In more recent years doubt has been cast upon the accuracy of the blue colour as GJ's locos were later painted green, though it is believed it may have been a special livery for the Paris exhibition. There is no doubt that she looks very attractive and it would be good to think that Nohab got it right back in the 1950s! She was placed on extended loan to GHJ in 1993 and has been kept at Hesselby ever since, latterly inside this frame at the back of the carriage shed. The plastic sheeting is used to wrap her up during the winter and a dehumidifier is used to provide additional protection from the elements. I saw her there on 26 July 2017. The intention is to keep her as a static exhibit in view of her historic significance and the amount of newly-manufactured material that that would be needed to put her back into working order. GJ went on to acquire a fascinating group of locos. The youngest and largest of them was their elegant 4-6-0 no 12 LÄRBRO, delivered by Nohab in 1920 and a close copy of no 24 and her sisters at VGJ.

The Klintehamn-Roma Järnväg opened in 1898 and served the south western part of Gotland. It closed in 1953, but that was not the end of the working career of its 0-6-0T no 1 KLINTEHAMN (Kristinehamn 59/1897), since SJ despatched her to the mainland in 1949 and she worked as the yard shunter at Växjö until she was withdrawn in 1961. Two years later she was placed in the care of Järnvägmuseet and put on display in a park at Målilla, close to the line between Växjö and Hultsfred. She moved to GHJ on loan in 1997 and the railway is currently running a fundraising appeal to restore her to working order. On 26 July 2017 she was kept at the back of the carriage shed along with GOTLAND. Her sister no 2 HÖFDINGEN (Kristinehamn 60/1897), was not so fortunate as she was withdrawn only one year after SJ took over in 1948 and was scrapped in 1950. Before it lost its independence GJ introduced railcars built by Hilding Carlsson, smaller and lighter than the YBo5p type, which were classified Yp by SJ. None of them have survived, but GHJ is building a replica using parts from a Danish standard gauge car. Another current project is the reconstruction of what was originally a steam railcar built by Wagonfabriken Arlov in 1910 for the Mönsterås Åseda Järnväg. It was converted at Kalmar to a i/c machine in 1932 and withdrawn in 1940. Its body was discovered some years ago and acquired by GHJ - a similar vehicle once ran on Gotland. Introduction of more diesels was a priority for SJ because of the poor quality of the island's water. Only a very few steam locos remained in use until the 1960 closures.

Back at Hesselby DALHEM has admirers as she takes water on 26 July 2017 before setting off on another journey to Roma. It turned out that I was lucky to see her in use during my visit, as a friend who was there a few days later found that she had been set aside for repair, and at the end of that season she was withdrawn in need of major attention to her boiler, work which is still under way in 2022. She is a very pretty loco and the railway is run by exceptionally friendly and helpful people. And … the smörgåsbord on offer at Eva and Ove's open-air café at Hesselby station was superb! Gotland occupies a strategic position within the Baltic Sea and was occupied by Russia in 1808 and again briefly in 1945. Since the start of the Ukrainian war Sweden's military forces have significantly increased their presence and if the country joins NATO many more troops are likely to be based there. We can but hope that the island's happy, laid-back character will not disappear.

Northern Gotland used to be dominated by limestone quarries, lime kilns and cement factories. For many years their product was exported to ports in mainland Sweden and further afield. Demand was particularly high late in the nineteenth century when large quantities of limestone were sent for use as a flux in blast furnaces in Germany and elsewhere. At that time there were about thirty quarries in the district, worked almost entirely with hand tools. During the twentieth century mechanisation increased, and an increasing proportion of the limestone was used to make cement. The kilns at Bläse date from the 1860s and were served by an isolated 891mm gauge system. Three of its five locos came secondhand from the Limhamn quarry railway. Lime burning ended in 1946 but the quarries continued to be worked for another ten years, after which the complex was donated to a charitable trust. It opened as a museum of the limestone industry in 1985. The site is dominated by two conical kilns and two unusually-shaped factory buildings, built of course of limestone. This one is now home to a 600mm gauge 0-4-0WT (O&K 12900/1937). She was supplied to a limeworks at Bungenäs, not far away, and in 1951 moved to another one at Smöjen where she worked until its railway closed in 1962. She was initially preserved at Hesselby and moved from there to Bläse. The local limestone has a distinctive grey colour and is still quarried; the road to Bläse passes through the enormous Storugn quarry complex, the largest anywhere in Scandinavia. 27 July 2017.

The Köping-Uttersberg Järnväg ran through Hedströmsdalen near the head of Mälaren, the lake which extends out from Stockholm into central Sweden. It was the railway whose gauge was altered from 3ft 6ins to 1093mm gauge in 1864 because of the confusion between British and Swedish measurements. If all had gone to plan it would have been Sweden's first public 3ft 6ins gauge railway, and only the second one anywhere in the world. It was built to serve the district's ironworks which were amongst the oldest in Sweden. Much of their product was exported by ship to Germany. Sea-going vessels could not enter Mälaren and Stockholm was established in the thirteenth century at the transhipment point. SJ took over the railway in 1952, and regauged seven of their small 891mm gauge Z4p class diesels in 1962 and 1963 to take over operations as the Z4tu class. The steam locos which they replaced were soon scrapped, but happily 0-6-0T no 7 PATRIC REUTERSWÄRD (Nohab 390/1894) escaped this fate as she had been sold back in 1958 to the Kohlswa ironworks for use on their private line to Guttsta, where it connected with KUJ. After SJ ceased operations in 1966 a short section at KUJ's northern end was taken over by the Riddarhytte steelworks, for which they bought two of the Z4tu locos, but it, too, closed in 1969. By then PATRIC REUTERSWÄRD had been out of a job for three years, but the loss of the final section aroused local interest in the line. She was presented to Köping council, and now lives in a purpose-built museum run by enthusiasts close to the old terminus at Köping harbour. Some of them very kindly opened it up for me when I visited on 21 September 2015.

Another view of PATRIC REUTERSWÄRD on 21 September 2015. Her new home was designed to resemble the old line's engine shed at Köping. She shares it with two KUJ carriages which have been beautifully restored, and with SJ no 316 (Kalmar 99/1952), one of the two 1,093mm gauge Z4tu diesels which had been sold to Riddarhytte steelworks in 1966. She is just visible on the right in this photo. After 1969 the two were sold on to the Nordmark-Klarälvens Järnväg (see pages 85-89) and altered back to 891mm gauge, and in preservation no 316, later NKIJ no 4, has had to be converted to 1,093mm a second time. The society has around two hundred metres of track at Köping harbour, overlooked both by the old railway company's offices and, a little further away, by a remarkably ornate house which it built for a former manager, an expense which it couldn't really afford. No 7's restoration has stalled until funds are raised to build a new firebox but once this is overcome the harbour should once again see a steam loco at work. Four more of the Z4tu diesels were converted back to 891mm gauge by SJ. One of them, no 397, had started life in Gotland and worked the last demolition trains there before moving to the mainland in 1963 and being converted to 1,093mm. After reverting to 891mm gauge she worked at Växjo, and returned to Gotland after being sold to GHJ in 1986. The ninth Z4tu, no 323, ended up as a 3ft 6ins gauge machine. She was unique in being the only loco to have run on all three of SJ's narrow gauges, but this wasn't enough to save her and she was scrapped in 1982.

Another former ironworks which has been preserved now forms the Surahammar Bruksmuseum in south eastern Bergslagen. The business opened in the early 1800's, and in about 1865 its owners won a contract to manufacture wheels for railway carriages and wagons. It has been making them ever since, now at a larger factory in another part of Surahammar. In 1876 a line was built which ran for about 10km from Lisjö to a quayside at a lock on the Strömsholm Canal in the town. Its main purpose was to bring in peat and timber as fuel for the furnaces, though it also carried passengers, especially at weekends. Often called Lisjöbanan it was at first stated to be 1,099mm gauge like the early lines further west in Bergslagen, but later a lengthy extension was proposed to join KUJ, and Lisjöbanan was then said to share its 1,093mm gauge. The idea was that the ironworks' product could be shipped via Köping harbour, but the connection was never built. The only loco was this tiny 0-4-0T VAULUNDER (Kristinehamn 17/1876) which ran until the railway closed in 1926. She was the only loco anywhere in Sweden to be fitted with Gooch valve gear. The old ironworks machinery, much of it specifically made or adapted for manufacturing the wheels, was left in situ and became a central part of the museum when it opened in the 1920s. It's a highly atmospheric place which still looks as though the workers have just gone home for the night and will be back tomorrow! In about 1928 VAULUNDER took up residence there together with a primitive carriage and a timber wagon. I saw them on 21 September 2015. Surahammar's modern steelworks now belongs to the Tata group. In addition to the railway wheels it has recently been chosen as their European plant for manufacturing specialist steel for electric vehicles in place of a steelworks in Wales, now a victim of Brexit.

The Kosta-Lessebo Järnväg, Sweden's first public 600mm gauge railway, opened in 1888 and was the line promoted by Axel Hummel, the ambitious manager of Kosta glassworks. He was appointed at a time when its fortunes were waning, and under his direction it began to work its extensive forests around the town for the sale of the timber rather than as fuel for its furnaces. The purpose of the railway was to carry it to the Kalmar Järnväg's main line at Lessebo. The Decauville 0-4-4-0 Mallet tender-tank machine which Mr Hummel had ordered in Paris back in 1887 was its first loco. Paul Decauville supplied three of these Mallets to Swedish railways, and he also licensed the design to Swedish builders and provided full sets of drawings, enabling them to build another four. These included KLJ's no 2 LESSEBO (Munktells 27/1891). Munktells built Sweden's first domestically-produced locos back in the 1850s and LESSEBO was their only Mallet. None of the country's seven public 600mm gauge railways survived into preservation, but they have a very worthy successor in the shape of the enthusiast-run Östra Södermanlands Järnväg, formed by a group of enthusiasts in 1959 as an offshoot of the Swedish Railway Club. Their first base was at Lina brickworks, near Södertälje and the line there became Sweden's first heritage operation. After the standard gauge branch to Mariefred, an old town on Mälaren, closed in 1964 they moved there and converted the branch to 600mm. A major part of their mission is to preserve as much of the surviving material from the seven railways as possible. Their collection was greatly enhanced when Järnvägmuseet entrusted them with LESSEBO in 2003. After initial assessment of her condition they started to restore her to working order, and here she is stripped down in their workshop at Mariefred on 30 July 2006.

Hummel went on to market Decauville's system and his locos. He was a consultant to the Nättraby-Alnaryd Järnväg, the line whose construction was first mooted in 1892 by one Axel E Lindvall. He encouraged its promoters to buy the Decauville-style Mallets, which were especially suited to lines with steep gradients and sharp curves though they were proving delicate and difficult to maintain. They thought otherwise, since their line was neither twisty nor hilly. Instead a specification for a modern 2-4-2T with the same 12-tonne weight was drawn up for them by Victor Klemming, a draftsman with SJ who later became the head of its machinery department. The result was a masterly design whose construction went out to tender, and Motala won the job. Six were built for three railways between 1894 and 1904. VIRÅ (Motala 272/1901) was no 2 of the Stavsjö Järnväg, a line built in a hurry to rescue timber from the Kolmården forest, near Norrköping, after it was blighted by disease. Virå is the name of its northern terminus. She has survived thanks to being sold as early as 1919 to A/S Bjørkåsen Gruber, a copper and sulphur mine at Ballangen, near Narvik in northern Norway, which opened in 1911. They reboiled her in 1939, and she continued to serve them until the mine closed in 1964. ÖSlJ acquired her the following year. A friend at Mariefred has described her as "a gem, YES; everybody's darling engine here. Steams beautifully and runs like an angel - better than any of our coaches do. Our max. permitted speed on the ÖSlJ is 15 mph - VIRÅ does 35 easily...". What more can I say?! Here she was standing on the morning of 26 September 2009 outside Mariefred engine shed.

The Jönköping–Gripenbergs Järnväg, which ran through the countryside to the east of Lake Vättern, was Sweden's third 600mm gauge railway when it opened in 1894. Its first locos were three Decauville-pattern Mallets which were only locos built by J & CG Bolinders, a large engineering firm based in Stockholm. It wasn't long before it needed something larger and more powerful, and from 1902 four 2-6-2Ts were supplied by Motala, who by then seem to have cornered the market for 600mm gauge locos. They were an enlarged version of their 2-4-2Ts like VIRÅ. The firm built two updated 2-6-2Ts in 1914 and 1915, one each for the Nättraby and Jönköping lines, with superheated boilers and outside Walschaerts valve gear. They were Europe's first superheated 600mm gauge locos, though both O&K and Jung followed suit within months. It is remarkable that Sweden progressed from importing its 600mm machines to becoming world leaders in their design within just twenty five years. After the First World War imports of cheap German-built locos and increasing road traffic brought this promising line of development to an end. Both the superheated 2-6-2Ts have survived and now live at ÖSlJ, thanks to having led second lives at Aspa Bruk after the demise of their original railways. Here no 4 KM NELSSON (Motala 520/1914), the Nättraby loco, arrives at Läggesta Nedre station on 21 July 2006.

Dag Bonnedal, who has been exceptionally helpful while I have been writing this book, is on the right of this photo and one of two crew members helping to turn KM NELSSON at Läggesta Nedre on 21 July 2006. She was purchased by Aspa Bruk in 1946, one year after the Nättraby line closed, and became their no 5. She joined JGJ no 9, the other superheated 2-6-2T which had moved to Aspa Bruk as their no 4, after JGJ closed in 1935. Aspa Bruk's forestry railway closed in 1951. Internal traffic continued for another twenty years, but it no longer needed the 2-6-2Ts and they went into store. In their very early years ÖSlJ attempted to buy both of them but were unsuccessful. KM NELSSON became a static exhibit in a park at Nässjö in 1963, and four years later she moved to ÖSlJ after they agreed to provide a standard gauge loco for the park in exchange.

On 21 July 2006 KM NELSSON has just set off for Mariefred from Läggesta Nedre station, which was known simply as Läggesta back in its standard gauge days. It lay on the main line between Stockholm, Södertälje and Eskilstuna, and was the junction for the branch to Mariefred, just 3.2km away. The bridge in the background of this photo carries Svealandsbanan, a high speed railway which replaced the old main line between between Södertälje and Eskilstuna in 1995. Shortly afterwards ÖSlJ took over the old railway from Läggesta as far as Taxinge, 7.5km to the east, and were still operating trains over it with a Y7 railcar when I first visited in 2006. Its conversion to 600mm gauge began in the following year, and it reopened in May 2011. The Nedre suffix to the station's name means "lower" and distinguishes it from the Svealandsbanan station.

KM NELSSON stands in front of Mariefred's fine old wooden station building and takes water on 21 July 2006. The building dates from the opening of the Mariefred branch line by the Norra Södermanlands Järnväg in 1895 along with its main line west from Södertälje, which at its greatest extent ran to Mälarbaden harbour, on the lake beyond Eskilstuna. Diesel railcars began operations on the branch in 1929. SJ took over in 1934 and both the branch and the main line were electrified two years later.

KM NELSSON and her train have set off from Mariefred on 21 July 2006 and have just passed ÖSlJ's engine shed and works which are to the left in this photo. The road over the level crossing leads to Gripsholms Slott, a magnificent medieval castle which occupies a promontory on the lake. The castle became a royal summer palace, though Sweden's monarchs have not lived there regularly since the eighteenth century. It is now open to the public as a museum and is also the home of Sweden's national portrait gallery. It was partly because of the large number of tourists who visit it that ÖSlJ chose to relocate from Lina to Mariefred. There is an unlikely connection between the founding of ÖSlJ and VAULUNDER at Surahammar with her Gooch valve gear. The gear was the subject of a question on a TV quiz show in the 1950s, and the interest this generated amongst enthusiasts led to the formation of the Swedish Railway Club, out of which ÖSlJ grew. No doubt Sir Daniel Gooch, the GWR's first locomotive engineer, later its long-serving chairman and a champion of Brunel's 7ft gauge, would have been amazed to learn of his contribution to 600mm gauge preservation in Sweden!

Another Brigadelok, but this time one that is in steam. In addition to the seven public railways in Sweden there were many industrial 600mm gauge systems. Eleven of the twelve Brigadeloks which went to the country after the First World War worked in industry. This loco, Hartmann 4290/1919, was another of the nine built in 1919 which must have arrived in Sweden brand new. She was bought by Emsfors Bruk, a paper mill near the Baltic coast between Västervik and Kalmar, to work on their railway which opened in 1920. The loco was generally known locally as THE BLUE after the colour she carried in her early years. She is now ÖSlJ's no 8 and carries her blue paintscheme once more. Nowadays she carries the name EMSFORS. Here she takes water at Mariefred station on 30 July 2006. The heavily-rebuilt semi-open coach to the left is one of several which JGJ used for its summer traffic and which doubled up as freight wagons, principally for the heavy traffic originating at Husqvarna Vapenfabrik, a large concern founded by the Swedish crown in 1689 for making rifles, which became privately-owned in 1757 and diversified after losing its rifle contract with the Crown in 1850. Its sewing machine business led to these vehicles becoming universally known as "sewing machine coaches". The earliest definite record of them is in 1925 when six were built, and more followed in later years. The railway was built largely to carry the traffic from the factory which was always its principal customer. Nowadays the pressure washers, chain saws and other outdoor power products it makes have made Husqvarna a household name around the world. It still uses a pictogram of a riflesight as its logo.

EMSFORS has finished her drink and stands at Mariefred station ready for departure on 30 July 2006. The Emsfors Bruk line connected the factory with a harbour at Påskallavik, and for a few years after 1920 there was also a siding which led to a peat bog south of Karlshammar. A second Brigadelok, also a Hartmann product, arrived in 1923 and was informally named THE GREEN after her first colour. The pair handled all traffic until a diesel took over in the early 1950s, after which THE BLUE was kept on as a reserve loco while THE GREEN went into store. The Emsfors Bruk line closed in 1975 and the track was lifted over the next few years, much of it being used to reconstruct the Böda forest line on Öland before it opened as Böda Skogsjärnväg. The paper company presented THE BLUE to ÖSlJ in 1969 and the THE GREEN in 1970 to the society which revived the Ohsabanan. The staff at Emsfors Bruk encouraged ÖSlJ to choose THE BLUE because it had been fitted with a new firebox in 1952 and its boiler was much better, whereas the Ohsabanan had to build a new one. Later it transpired that its motion was in poorer shape than that on THE GREEN, so perhaps the Ohsabanan didn't do too badly after all!

EMSFORS heads through the countryside near Marielund on 30 July 2006 with a train bound for Läggesta Nedre. Only one Brigadelok found her way to a public railway in Sweden, No. 3 at the Munkedals Järnväg, on the west coast north of Gothenburg, which was built mainly to serve another paper mill. Their loco was built by Borsig in 1919 and was sold to the railway by Nohab in 1925. Despite her small wheels and boiler and the complications of her Klien-Lindner articulation she appears to have been well-used. In 1940 she was withdrawn and in the following year was replaced by a O&K 2-6-2T which had been built for the Stavsjö Järnväg in 1920 to the same general specifications as the Motala ones, and which served the Stavsjö line until it closed in 1939. ÖSlJ has found that EMSFORS cannot run comfortably at any greater speed than 20kph and when she is in traffic her small boiler needs careful nurturing – quite a contrast to the free-steaming and speedy VIRÅ and the 2-6-2Ts from Motala. Some of those at ÖSlJ wondered whether she would be able to cope with the demands posed by the extension to Taxinge, but she has surprised them and continues to be a much-valued loco, able to keep to schedule provided she is not expected to make up time in the event of delay. She retains her Klien-Lindner articulation.

Although Gripsholms Slott lies only a few hundred metres away from ÖSlJ I found it difficult to include it in a train photo, at least on a sunny day, as it involved shooting into the sun during most of the railway's operating hours. There has been a castle on the site since the 1300s, though the present structure mostly dates from a radical reconstruction in 1537. It is an absolutely fascinating building, with elaborately decorated interiors reflecting various eras between the sixteenth and nineteenth centuries. Parts were rebuilt in the late nineteenth century in what has always been a somewhat controversial attempt to make the building look older than it really is, but fortunately much of it was left alone, including the castle's pocket-sized theatre, completed in 1781 to occupy one of the round towers. The auditorium is sumptuously decorated but perhaps the most intriguing area is backstage where all the machinery for moving the sets remains just as it was after the last known performance took place there just four years later. It is almost certainly the most complete theatre from the period anywhere in Europe, rather more so than the better-known one at the Drottningholm palace in the outskirts of Stockholm. Here the castle forms a backdrop as EMSFORS heads away from Mariefred in the early evening of 30 July 2006 after the sun had moved round sufficiently to make this angle possible. The attractive leading coach, JGJ no 11, is one of three large-platform ones built by the Kosta Mekaniska Verkstad, founded in 1898 by Axel Hummel as an offshoot of KLJ and the Kosta glassworks. No 11 was built in 1903. It and JGJ's similar coach no 12 went first to HRRJ and were acquired by JGJ when HRRJ was converted to standard gauge. Both now run on ÖSlJ. The third spent its working life on KLJ and ÖSlJ now owns its frame.

For more than fifty years ÖSlJ has held a gala late in September to mark the close of its operating season. The 2009 event on was notable for being the first during which all four surviving steam locos from the country's seven public railways could be seen together in steam. Getting there involved setting off from home soon after 3.00am for the flight to an airport near Mariefred. I arrived not long after sunrise in time to see the locos being prepared outside the shed for their day's activities. On the left is LESSEBO whose restoration to working order had been completed earlier in the year. Beyond her is VIRÅ, which did not see much use on that occasion as her firebox was approaching the end of its working life. On the right is 0-4-0T no 1 LOTTA (O&K 6620/1913). She was originally SJ's no BYCF 11 and was used on construction work for the doubling of some of its main lines in southern Sweden. In 1928 she was sold to the Kohlswa steelworks for use on their 4km line from Åkerby feldspar mine to Torp station on the Köping-Uttersbergs line, until the Åkerby line closed in 1955. She became ÖSlJ's first loco in 1959 and was their only working one during their first year at Lina. In 1990 she was set aside in need of boiler work and she became an exhibit at Tekniska Museet at Stockholm in 1996. When I took this photo on 26 September 2009 she had just returned to Mariefred. Since then she has been overhauled and she returned to service in 2019.

LESSEBO stands at Mariefred station on 26 September 2009. Behind her is 0-4-4-0 Mallet tank no 5 HAMRA (O&K 930/1902), one of two of her builders' small Mallet locos to run in Sweden. O&K built these locos in considerable numbers, mainly for sugar factories in Java. This loco was supplied to AB Separator, which manufactured milk separating machines and other dairy equipment at Tumba, south west of Stockholm, and also ran an experimental dairy farm at Hamra Gård nearby. She worked on a 600mm gauge line about 5km long to Tumba station on the Stockholm-Södertälje-Eskilstuna line, after 1925 in the company of a Brigadelok which came secondhand from the Stockholm city port. The Hamra line closed in 1946, and the Mallet was sold in the following year to Ahr limestone quarry in northern Gotland, where she enjoyed a reunion with the Brigadelok which had moved there in 1943. She was rescued in the nick of time in 1961, just before cutting up was due to begin, in a deal which required ÖSlJ to provide a O&K 0-4-0T in exchange. The 0-4-0T was subsequently scrapped together with the Brigadelok. The other Mallet, an identical machine, was a stablemate of LESSEBO at KLJ. The dark blue coach on the left is no 1 from the Munkedals Järnväg. Although the seven public railways all closed long before ÖSlJ was formed many coaches survived as summer houses or shooting lodges. Seven of them, one from each of the seven public railways, were acquired and meticulously restored by 1971, and since then have been followed by three more. Four more historic coaches have been reconstructed using varying amounts of original material. Amongst 600mm gauge lines worldwide probably only the Ffestiniog Railway in Wales can boast a similar number of fully-restored historic vehicles.

When Aspa Bruk disposed of the two superheated 2-6-2Ts in 1963 JGJ no 9 (Motala 568/1915) went to a museum at Skärstad, near Huskvarna, the town where the Husqvarna plant is located, and remained there until she moved to ÖSlJ on long term loan in 2006. On 26 September 2009 she was making her first public appearance after restoration to working order. Here no 9 and KM NELSSON prepare to leave Mariefred station with a freight train. The diesel hiding coyly behind the trees to the right was built by Deutz for Aspa Bruk in 1923, and ran there until 1970. The battery loco partially visible on the left with the varnished wooden bodywork was built by ASEA in 1916 and spent her working life on a 600mm gauge industrial line built back in 1895 to connect Garphyttan Bruk, an ironworks, with the Örebro–Svartå main line at Latorpsbruk. It closed in 1965 and the loco was acquired by Svenska Spårvägssällskapet, a tram preservation society. She moved to ÖSlJ three years later, still carrying her original batteries. ÖSlJ replaced them with some from a SJ standard gauge loco which probably date from about 1950.

In 1970 ÖSlJ extended its running line from Mariefred station to a jetty on Mälaren. The ducks are unperturbed by the passage of the train on 26 September 2009 as they paddle peacefully on the lake! The brown coach is one of two closed ones built by Decauville for the Helsingborg-Råå-Ramlösa Järnväg in 1898 which are now the only Decauville-built 600mm gauge bogie carriages to have survived anywhere in the world. The HRRJ was the line whose promoter, one Fredrik Posse, visited Paris in 1889 and bought some of Decauville's equipment second-hand after the exhibition railway there closed. The HRRJ opened in 1891 and was so successful that it outgrew the capacity of the Decauville equipment and was converted to a standard gauge electric interurban railway in 1906. Two of its Decauville locos, one Mallet and one of the firm's later 0-6-2Ts, and these two carriages along with ten wagons, were all bought by the Anneberg-Ormaryds Järnväg. It opened in 1909 and was the last of the seven public railways to be built. Another HRRJ loco, the only Decauville 0-4-2T to reach Sweden, went to the Ohs line. A second Decauville 0-6-2T went new to the JGJ. No Decauville-built loco has survived in Sweden, though the frame and running gear, including the side rods, of Decauville no 58, only the second Mallet to be built anywhere, were heavily reconstructed as a petrol loco. It belongs to ÖSlJ and is currently on loan to the Frövi museum. The only survivor anywhere of the 0-6-2Ts ran on the Pithiviers museum railway south of Paris until her boiler certificate expired in 2020. Out of four 0-4-2Ts which worked on Queensland's sugar railways one now runs on the Bredgar & Wormshill Railway in Kent and two await restoration in Australia.

The extension to the harbour terminates next to this pretty old steam boat station building. It serves the SS MARIEFRED, a coal-fired steamship which was built in 1903 at Södra Varfvet in Stockholm, the site of which now forms the Viking Line dock from where ferries leave for Mariehamn in the Åland Islands, Helsinki, Turku and Tallinn. MARIEFRED has plied the route between Stockholm and Mariefred continuously since then, probably the longest period that one route has been served by the same ship anywhere in the world, and has been operated by the same company since 1905. The service ceased to be profitable in the early 1930s and in 1936 the company was taken over by three Mariefred businessmen and the ship's captain, simply to keep it running without any expectation of making a profit. In 1966 they handed over to a preservation society which also operates two smaller steam vessels serving the Stockholm archipelago. The society has run the Mariefred service ever since and provides funds to cover its operating loss. MARIEFRED leaves Klara Mälarstrand in central Stockholm every day in midsummer and at weekends until mid-September. With a maximum speed of only ten knots she is no speedster and the voyage lasts three and a half hours. She sometimes makes a side trip between Mariefred and Taxinge before beginning her return sailing to Stockholm late in the afternoon. The railway generally runs a train through to the harbour to collect arriving passengers. On 30 July 2006 MARIEFRED had just left the jetty at Mariefred and was turning before heading for Taxinge.

The extension is about 500m long and has a distinctly different character from the rest of the railway. EMSFORS waits to set off from the harbour with a freight train on 26 September 2009. Freight was the principal traffic for most of the seven public railways and ÖSlJ has assembled a large collection of wagons from all of them. EMSFORS needed modification to make her suitable for service on a public railway, but happily the alterations were relatively minor, and she is still unmistakeably a Brigadelok. MUNKEDAL was modified in much the same way before she began service on the Munkedals Järnväg. Within the last few years this part of the lake shore has been gentrified, and a boardwalk-type structure has been erected to the right of the railway track.

On 26 September 2009 EMSFORS and her freight train pass the oldest part of Mariefred, overlooked by its fine medieval stone church or kyrka. It was built between 1621 and 1624 over the ruins of an old Carthusian monastery but was partly destroyed by fire in 1682 and was rebuilt and consecrated for a second time in 1697. Most of the old houses in the town are made of wood, but medieval churches in Sweden were generally built of stone and wooden ones are unusual. The building is widely regarded as one of the most significant architectural treasures within the Diocese of Strängnäs. The current organ was built in 1983 by Mats Arvidsson, a widely-respected Swedish organ builder. It became well-known amongst lovers of JS Bach's music when the church was amongst those chosen just three years later as one of the venues for a recording of a complete set of his organ works performed by the Danish organist Hans Fagius. The red-painted wooden buildings nearer the railway are part of Callanderska Gården, Mariefred's local history museum.

EMSFORS sets off from Mariefred for Läggesta Nedre on 26 September 2009. The HRRJ connected Helsingborg, on the narrowest part of the Kattegat opposite Helsingør in Denmark, with a beach at Råå and a health resort and spa at Ramlösa, to the south of the town. In summer there was much demand for open coaches like the leading one in this photo. The first two were built by Decauville in 1889 and were amongst the stock bought secondhand from the Paris exhibition. Four generally similar ones came from Helsingborgs Mekaniska Verkstad three years later. This replica incorporates the original bogies of one of them, and is one of five replica coaches built by the ÖSlJ incorporating some original parts, which supplement its original coaches from the old railways. The second coach was no 4 came from the Nättraby line from VABIS in 1910 and was the very last coach to be built for any of the Swedish 600mm railways. By then the line had been extended and was officially known as the Nättraby-Alnaryd-Elmeboda Järnväg, though it was popularly called the Krösnabanan, supposedly because its trains were so slow that passengers could jump off, pick wild berries at the lineside and climb back on. Just visible behind it is NAEJ no 3.

KM NELSSON heads away from Mariefred on 26 September 2009 with another train for Läggesta Nedre. The leading coach, with its attractive pale blue paint scheme, is KLJ no 103. This railway began its passenger service in 1891 with a single coach, no 101, from Decauville. No 103 was built two years later by Dolbergs of Rostock. It looks more German than French, though it was in some respects a fairly straightforward copy of no 101, and was ordered soon after a study visit to Kosta by a group from Rostock. When KLJ closed in 1948 it was presented to Järnvägmuseet and moved on to ÖSIJ when it first opened at Lina in 1959, initially on loan but the railway later acquired it outright. It originally had a large third class compartment and a smaller second class one, together with a luggage section which was separated from the passenger accommodation by an open platform, a typical arrangement for German carriages of the period. In 1905 the luggage compartment was replaced by ladies-only accommodation. The vehicle's noticeable sag has been a feature for many years and results from structural weaknesses inherent in the original Decauville concept.

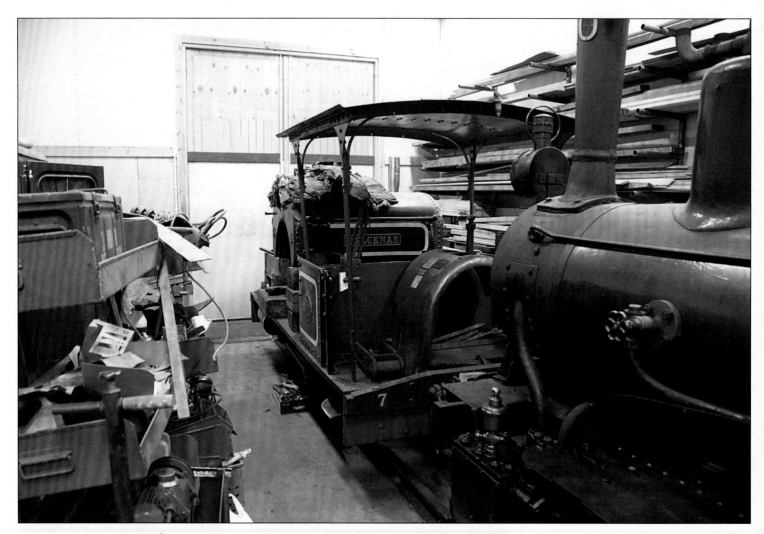

Eds Bruk's no 1 HELGENÄS, the tiny 0-4-2ST built by Hudswell Clarke in 1889 for the Eds Bruk railway and the elder sister of no 3 at Linköping (see page 39), saw occasional use at Mariefred until her boiler became too tired in 2000. She is the oldest surviving Hudswell Clarke loco anywhere in the world. When I saw her on 26 September 2009 her boiler had been removed, but no other work on her was done while ÖSlJ's volunteer effort concentrated on setting up and consolidating the extension to Taxinge. Now the railway hopes to begin her restoration in the near future. She was positively dwarfed by the 0-6-0T in the foreground (O&K 10549/1923), one of group of three 5-tonne 0-6-0Ts ordered by the Crown forestry office which by normal standards would be considered to be small machines. This loco worked on a forest railway on Hunneberg mountain, northeast of Trollhättan, which was being adapted from an old peat railway, the timber being taken down the mountainside by a cableway to Lilleskog station on UVHJ, by then a standard gauge line (see page 21). The forest railway closed in about 1937 and in 1944 she began a second life as Avesta steelworks no 6, latterly in the company of sister loco no 3 from which she acquired her boiler and cab. She was withdrawn in 1954 and arrived at ÖSlJ in 1986. Both locos were being stored at the back of the workshop at Mariefred, squeezed in between racks of spare parts and materials! Since my visit the 0-6-0T has been restored, though like HELGENÄS she is insufficiently powerful for regular service.

It is early evening at Läggesta Nedre on 26 September 2009 and LESSEBO is being turned before taking the last train back to Mariefred on this excellent gala day. KLJ was the only Swedish line whose traffic was worked exclusively by Mallets for the whole of its life, its only conventional loco being a small Decauville 0-4-0T shunter. The Munkedals Järnväg was in need of a new loco in 1948 to handle traffic for the expanding Munkedals paper factory, just as KLJ closed and LESSEBO was facing a most uncertain future. She was the only 600mm loco available for purchase anywhere in Sweden which was already certified for use on a public railway, and the trouble this saved MJ earned her an unexpected reprieve. The certification for public service still applied when she returned to service in 2009 and so saved ÖSlJ the same trouble! The antiquated machine must have made an unusual sight hauling trains of the modern oil tankers in use on the Munkedals line, and it was perhaps ironic that a Decauville-designed Mallet from Sweden's first public 600mm line should also serve its last surviving one. She was set aside in 1954, shortly before MJ was converted to standard gauge, and by then LESSEBO's historic significance was appreciated. She was acquired by Järnvägsmuseet, and remained there until her loan to ÖSlJ began. She made occasional outings after her restoration was completed in 2009, but is currently a static exhibit.

In 1885 the Stockholm-Rimbo Järnvägsaktiebolag opened the first section of the 891mm gauge system running out from Stockholm Östra station into the Roslagen district northeast of the city. It wasn't long before extensions were built and other railways were acquired; some of these were older than SRJ, the earliest being the Uppsala-Länna Järnväg which opened in 1874. It served the district to the east of Uppsala, the home of Sweden's principal university and the provincial capital of Uppland province which once included much of Stockholm. The SRJ company officially kept the Stockholm-Rimbo Järnvägsaktiebolag name until it was nationalised in 1951, though in 1909 for its everyday operations it adopted the name Stockholm-Roslagens Järnväg which conveniently had the same initials! No 3 RIMBO (Nohab 195/1884) was one of three locos supplied for the opening of its first line and the last of them to remain in service. She was withdrawn in 1923 and presented to Järnvägmuseet in 1930, but stayed at the railway until 1942 and worked once more in 1935 to celebrate its fiftieth anniversary. This delightful machine is typical of many locos built for Sweden's 891mm gauge railways in the 1880s. On 14 July 2016 she was standing in Järnvägmuseet's storage roundhouse. To the left is one of Sweden's very few 891mm gauge private saloons, and beyond it is the 891mm Nordmark-Klarälvens Järnväg electric loco no 44, one of fifteen built by AEG in Berlin in 1920 and 1921. The whole of the old Uppsala-Länna Järnväg is now a heritage railway which uses the same name, and also includes a later section running eastwards from Länna to Faringe. RIMBO recently moved from Gävle to its engine shed at Faringe and it is hoped to restore her to working order. ULJ is popularly called Lennakatten, supposedly from the wheezing, cat-like sound made by a steam railcar which once ran on the old railway.

The little 891mm gauge 4-4-0T NANNA (Nohab 464/1897) was built for the Kalmar-Berga Järnväg as their no 5. In 1915 she moved to the Mönsterås–Åseda Järnväg, which connected with KBJ at Sandbäckshult, and was sold only three years later to SRJ. She was their no 35 and in 1935 moved into industrial service at a quarry at Dannemora, near the northern end of the SRJ system. She stayed there until entering preservation in 1967, first at Kalmar and from 1968 at Anten. Throughout all her working life she carried her original name which is that of a Nordic goddess. A superbly restored 4-wheeled carriage from MÅJ is kept at ULJ. 4 August 2015.

SRJ operated the second largest 891mm network anywhere in Sweden. No 28 (Henschel 17607/1920) was one of three 2-6-2s known as the "Stortyskarna" or "Big Germans", which were the youngest of its steam locos and also the heaviest ones to run anywhere on the 891mm gauge. Here she stands in a shed at Faringe on 21 July 2006. She had operated on the line until the early 2000s, and as I write this is being overhauled. SRJ was nationalised in 1951 and became a part of SJ in 1959. They renumbered its electrics and diesels but not the remaining steam locos whose working lives were almost over. They were withdrawn between 1960 and 1962, replaced on the non-electric lines by the Yp railcars, the small Z4p and the larger Tp locos, along with two T2p class machines specially built for SRJ in 1958. After 1960 no 28 was stored at Faringe engine shed until moving to Järnvägsmuseet in 1970. She has been on loan to ULJ since 1987. It is a matter of regret that she is the only survivor of SRJ's later steam locos. Much of its suburban traffic was handled very competently by a group of 2-6-2Ts in the years before electrification and they would have been excellent performers on Sweden's heritage railways. SRJ once reached Lövsta Bruk, 160km north of Stockholm; short sections had been pruned since the 1930s and large-scale closures began in 1960. The first section of SRJ out of Stockholm as far as Djursholm became one of the world's first electrified lines in 1895. The wires reached Rimbo in 1946 and Norrtälje, a large town on the coast, in 1949, but the last train beyond Rimbo ran just twenty years later.

BLJ's 2-8-0 no 5 THOR (Falun 107/1909) was the working loco on both the occasions I have visited ULJ. She is identical to SRJ's 2-8-0 no 18, which was built in 1906 and wasn't scrapped until 1961, and so she presents a pleasingly authentic appearance whenever she runs there. THOR has run almost continuously at ULJ for more than forty five years, usually putting in about 6,000km annually, and is undoubtedly the top performer amongst all Sweden's preserved steam locos. She is a great credit to ULJ's engineers, and also to BLJ which maintained its locos to a high standard right up to its closure. Here she approaches Almunge station on the afternoon of 21 July 2006. One of SRJ's oldest lines, the long one between Dannemora and Hargshamn which opened back in 1878, was converted to standard gauge between 1950 and 1960. Further south what remained of the system was transferred in 1971 from SJ to Greater Stockholm's transport authority and renamed Roslagsbanan, but the closures continued and at one stage there was a serious proposal to shut it down altogether. Fortunately it was saved thanks to an overwhelming vote in a referendum in 1980, but this did not prevent the closure of the main line north from Kårsta to Rimbo in the following year. Trains still run as far as Kårsta, out in the countryside 41km from Stockholm Östra, and there are shorter branches to Österskär and Näsbypark. A decision has been taken in principle to reconstruct the line to Rimbo, but no funding has yet been allocated. Roslagsbanan's electric suburban services now see some of the heaviest railway traffic anywhere in the country, and the lines are all equipped with modern signalling and centralised train control.

THOR was working tender-first on her return trip to Uppsala with a late afternoon train on 21 July 2006. Here she has arrived at Marielund, midway along the line, and is crossing a former YBo5p railcar and trailer. Five of these railcars were converted to 3ft 6ins gauge in the 1960s to replace older cars which were worn out and becoming unreliable, and there was a surplus of 891mm lines after line closures. The light weight and good performance of the YBo5p cars was attributed to the use of an epicyclic gearbox and fluid coupling of British origin, manufactured by Daimler and Vulcan Sinclair. The epicyclic box was developed by Major WG Wilson for use in tanks during the First World War. SRJ's no 18 was one of three identical 2-8-0's which Falun built in 1906 for the Dala-Ockelbo-Norrsundet Järnväg (see pages 91-98), but was diverted to SRJ. A replacement was supplied to DONJ in 1907 to complete its order and lasted there until in 1968; one might have hoped that she would have been saved since the society which went on to preserve a short section of DONJ had already been established at Jädraås, its operating centre. Instead she was scrapped and THOR is the only survivor of the five 2-8-0s. She was BLJ's only tender loco, was plinthed at Långshyttan in 1966 and moved to ULJ in 1974.

At Almunge the final section of the line turns abruptly to the north towards Faringe and climbs through a low range of hills. In the early evening of 14 July 2016 THOR has left Almunge and passes Moga. The leading coaches in her train are two of a series of teak-clad ones built by ASEA for SRJ in 1914. SRJ introduced transporter wagons in 1955, with transfer facilities at Uppsala, and offered a through service to Norrtälje and Hallstavik, the home of one of Sweden's largest paper factories. Freight traffic increased enormously and the locos hitherto used in freight service often stalled while working the heavy trains on this section. When the Big Germans were ousted from their express passenger duties by electrification they found a new role working these freight trains. However their reign was brief and Tp class 2-6-2 diesels took over from them in 1958. Twenty five of these locos were built for SJ in 1953 and 1954 and initially worked in Västergötland and Småland. They were distinctive because of their rod drive, their unusual shape and their bright green paintscheme in place of the dull red/brown colour which SJ usually applied to its diesels and electrics in those days. Fifteen were rebuilt as standard gauge 0-8-0s in the mid-1960s, losing the green livery in the process. Four of the ones which remained as narrow gauge machines have been preserved, including no 3515 at ULJ. She was one of the locos which worked the Hallstavik traffic after the demise of the Big Germans until the standard gauge line between Dannemora and Hargshamn was extended to the town in 1977. The two T2p locos followed their design but ran on bogies and had more conventional-looking bodies.

This pretty little loco is the 802mm gauge Striberg-Grängens Järnväg's 2-6-0T no 4 (Nohab 249/1887). The railway opened in 1887 and in 1893 was amalgamated with others to form the 97km Bredsjö-Degerfors Järnväg. It was owned by the standard gauge Nora-Karlskoga Järnväg which was the subject of a merger in 1905 and became the Nora Bergslagen Järnväg. Most of BDJ was converted to standard gauge in 1907, but a 10km section which served an iron ore mine at Dalkarlsberg remained narrow gauge, mainly because NBJ knew that with its odd gauge the resale value of the stock would be minimal and without a good sale price the conversion would not have been cost-effective. No 4 was one of three locos which were kept on until this final section closed in 1953. They were maintained at NBJ's works at Nora, to which they were carried on standard gauge wagons, and in 1954 no 4 was preserved at Nora station, nowadays the operating base of a standard gauge heritage line. She is exhibited, along with two beautifully restored BDJ coaches, in a small museum housed in the station's old goods shed, and I saw them there on 22 September 2015.

The other main public 802mm line in western Bergslagen, the Säfsnäs Järnväg, was built from 1875, with its operating base at Fredriksberg. Extensions included a branch to Neva on Inlandsbanan, the 1,288km line between Kristinehamn, on the northern shore of Lake Vänern, and Gällivare in the far north of Sweden, which was built between 1908 and 1937 as a strategic route away from the coast and to open up some of the vast forests in the north of Sweden., but is today mostly a tourist railway. Other extensions and takeovers culminated in the opening in 1930 of a long line to Hällefors, home of a large ironworks, whereupon it was renamed the Hällefors-Fredriksberg Järnvägar. It route lay only a short distance from the Bredsjö railway but they never joined up. Closures began in 1940 and the last trains ran in 1970. Much of the HFJ's passenger traffic after 1932 was handled by a splendid Volvo-built railbus which still operates, now as a 600mm gauge vehicle on ÖSlJ. This beefy-looking 2-8-2T, no 7 KNUT FALK (Helsingborg 59/1920) is one of four survivors of the line's ten steam locos. She became an exhibit at Helsingborg Museum between 1966 and 1994, after which she moved to Skara engine shed where I saw her on 4 August 2015. Other railways to the south were initially proposed as 802mm gauge lines, but like the pioneering Hjo-Stenstorps Järnväg those which eventually reached fruition were built as parts of the Västergötland 891mm system.

The 1099 mm gauge loco from the pioneering Frykstad railway (Munktells 2/1855), the country's oldest surviving loco, was rightly enjoying pride of place at Järnvägmuseet on 14 July 2016. She carried neither a name nor a number when in service. The name was added when she moved to the newly-established Järnvägmuseet in 1906, but the spelling is a mistake. The coach partially visible to her right was built in 1859 when King Charles XV made a trip over the 8km-long line behind her. According to the English-language edition of the museum's guidebook he "enjoyed the chase, and considered both four-footed creatures and pretty women fair game" and "many people in the country districts of Sweden can consider themselves descendants." The vehicle's end windows "which were considered an unheard-of luxury, must have made it easier for His Majesty to keep a close eye on the passing hunting grounds." Who am I to disagree?! The Frykstad railway connected Lake Fryken with Klarälven. It became redundant when a standard gauge main line opened close by, and the loco began a brief second career on construction work on fortresses at Karlskrona and Karlsborg. FÖRSTLINGEN, Munktells' and the country's first loco, was converted to standard gauge after her brief and unsuccessful career as an 891mm machine. She worked on construction of the Nora-Ervalla Järnväg, which opened in 1856 and today is part of the Nora standard gauge heritage line. She was scrapped in 1882 save for a few parts which are now preserved and there is a replica of her in her standard gauge form at the Munktells museum in Eskilstuna. Munktells Mekaniska Verkstad, to use its full name, was founded in 1832. The thirty one steam locos it built between 1853 and 1900 formed only a small part of its output which for many years consisted mainly of the 6,535 traction engines which left its gates between 1854 and 1921. It later built tractors and is now the oldest constituent of the Volvo concern. Its factory at Eskilstuna is still in use.

Uddeholms AB, an iron and steel business which has traded in several locations around Hagfors, dates back to the 1600s. In 1874 it opened an internal 891mm gauge railway between Taberg and Motjärnhyttan, and public services began in 1877. More lines followed, and eventually they all became part of the 175km-long Nordmark-Klarälvens Järnväg. No 1 UA was built by Henry Hughes in 1874. As with Hughes's 1878 Corris Railway locos UA's original 0-4-0ST configuration was unsatisfactory. NKIJ adopted the sane cure as the Corris, and UA acquired a trailing axle by 1879. She was set aside in 1919 after some years shunting at Stjärnsfors, and spent a final spell on construction work at Munkfors steelworks between 1925 and 1930. Here she stands at the NKIJ's excellent museum at Hagfors on 22 September 2015. Although she's been an exhibit ever since 1931 oil or water seems still to be dripping from her cylinders, though this is probably just a consequence of being moved around the museum from time to time. Behind her is 0-6-2T no 5 LOVISA TRANÆA (Avonside 1114/1875). Both locos were reboilered by Nohab in 1902 when they perhaps acquired their typically Swedish turbine spark arresters. The farthest steam loco is 0-6-2T no 7 HAGFORS (Nohab 175/1883). The origin of UA's name is unclear. It may simply stand for Uddeholms AB, or it may perhaps be an early or dialectal form of the name of the River Uvån which flows through Hagfors. NKIJ's main line was electrified between 1921 and 1942. The brown electric loco in the background is no 33, one of the fifteen machines built by AEG in 1920 and 1921 like no 44 at Järnvägmuseet (see page 76). The red and cream one is no 102 MUNKFORS, from a group of six which came from ASEA between 1961 and 1966.

A rear view of LOVISA TRANÆA on 22 September 2015. The loco was originally named KLARAN, the later name being that of the wife of the owner of the Uddeholms company in the early 1700s. She was fitted with larger tanks and a rear bunker by Nohab in 1890 and 1891. She still carries the paint applied during her final overhaul before she was withdrawn in 1954. She became a resident of the museum in 1956. The vehicle beyond UA is described in Swedish as a landsvägslokomotiv or a highway locomotive. Uddeholms prepared its first railway scheme in 1858 to replace its previous barge transport but the project did not reach fruition and the landsvägslokomotiv was bought as a possible alternative. She was built in 1861 by Tuxford & Sons of Skirbeck, near Boston, Lincolnshire. They were agricultural engineers who built portable steam engines from 1850 and their first traction engines later in that decade. She was tried out in 1862 but was deemed to be a failure because of the poor state of the local roads and soon became a stationary power source for a crane used to tranship coal at Edebäck. She survived to become a museum exhibit, initially at Stjärnsfors, and has been at the Hagfors museum since 1988. The brown electric loco is again no 33.

Like TROLLHÄTTAN in the Innovatum museum HAGFORS, the Nohab-built loco, was largely a copy of a previous British design, in this case that of LOVISA TRANÆA and her sisters. In 1909 and 1910 she was rebuilt by Nohab as a superheated loco but photos taken over the subsequent years suggest that she was never fitted with the usual turbine spark arrester. She moved to Munkfors steelworks in 1957 and returned ten years later to join the collection at the Hagfors museum. Standing behind HAGFORS is an electric railcar, the survivor of two three-car sets built by Hilding Carlsson for NKIJ in 1956 which in their day were the fastest railcars anywhere on the 891mm gauge. The brown vehicle on the left is steam railcar no 1, described and illustrated on pages 88 and 89. The electrification of NKIJ wasn't enough to keep it going after the iron and steel traffic died away. Passenger services ended in 1964 and its last narrow gauge section, between Hagfors and a junction with SJ at Deje, closed completely in 1990, though a line between Karlstad and Skoghall, which was converted to mixed standard/891mm gauge in 1938, still sees standard gauge traffic and was taken over by SJ in 1991. The 891mm track between Hagfors and Stjärnsfors remains in situ and there are occasional suggestions that it should become a heritage railway. 22 September 2015. This would be a really valuable project if it were to come to fruition, especially if some of the machines in the museum were restored to operate it.

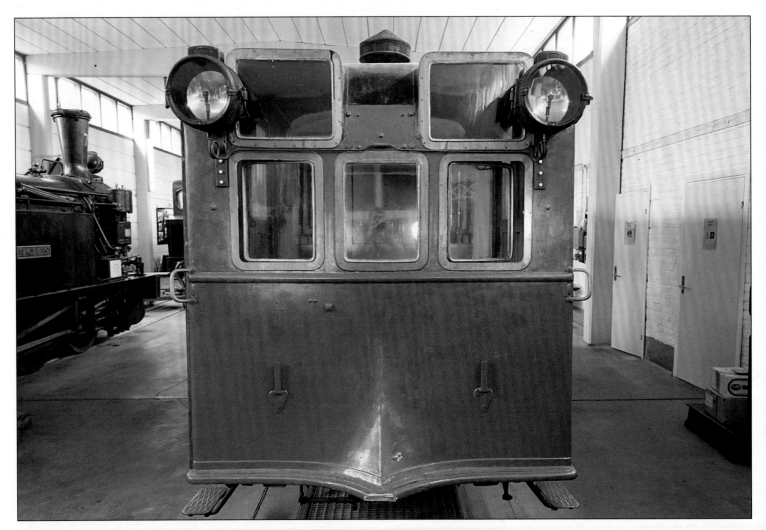

This optimistically streamlined steam railcar, NKlJ's no 1 (Wallberg och Lundvik 10/1900), is one of two which the firm built for the line at their factory at Vänersborg, near Trollhättan. It's a shame that she is missing the tip of her nose! Her paintwork is that which she carried when she was withdrawn in 1937 and took up residence in the Hagfors museum. Her sister no 2 was built in 1919 and eventually scrapped. Several 891mm gauge railways acquired similar steam railcars in the late 1800s and early 1900s. 22 September 2015.

This is a view of the engine compartment of railcar no 1 with its vertical boiler on 22 September 2015, still looking much as it must have done when she completed her last journey. On many Swedish railways these vehicles seem to have been used primarily as service or inspection vehicles, and on the longer, more remote lines, to convey medical staff in case of emergency. The Hagfors museum is based in the NKIJ's old railcar shed and in the adjoining roundhouse, a steam-era building which now houses coaches and wagons. The track in the yard looks unchanged from the railway's working years. The steelworks next to it is still very much in use as Uddeholms has concentrated its production there. It is nowadays noted as a world leader in the manufacture of steels for industrial tools. The whole site retains an authentic railway-like atmosphere and forms a worthy memorial to the old line – so much so that it is easy to half-expect that an electric loco will come trundling past with a train of iron ore or steel products!

BLJ ran south from a junction with SJ at Byvalla to Långshyttan, which was its operating base and the home of its engine shed. No 2 KLOSTER (Nohab 303/1890) was named after the Kloster ironworks concern which owned the railway and ran several plants around Långshyttan, Born and Stjärnsund. She was probably the smallest of the railway's five 0-6-0Ts and was initially used on an older railway between Långshyttan and Born-Engelsfors which was replaced by BLJ in 1891. She became BLJ's most venerable machine in 1913 after no 1 OSCAR, a 0-4-2T built by Kristenhamn in 1880 which it inherited from the Born-Engelsfors line, was transferred to internal service at Kloster ironworks. KLOSTER was withdrawn in about 1957 and found a home in what is now the Kloster ironworks museum at Långshyttan after spending some years in store at the back of the engine shed in the town. Altogether six of BLJ's eleven locos survived to be preserved thanks to the transfer of three of them to internal service at the Långshyttan ironworks after the 1964 closure, but KLOSTER is the only one still at her old home. She lives upstairs in an old wooden building and getting her there must have presented an interesting challenge! The curator was very upset that her dome cover had been stolen shortly before when I visited on 13 July 2016.

The 891mm gauge Dala-Ockelbo-Norrsundet Järnväg ran through Gästrikland and eastern Dalarna, effectively the north eastern part of the same iron ore district as that served by NKlJ, BLJ and the Bergslagen 802mm gauge lines. It connected Linghed with the Baltic coast at Norrsundet, 86km away, and was built in stages between 1875 and 1897. Jädraås and Ockelbo were the two principal intermediate stations and from the start Jädraås was the home of its workshops and its main engine shed. Initially the principal traffic was iron ore, from a mine at Vintjärn, and timber and charcoal from the vast woods, at first to provide fuel for the ironworks along the route but later for despatch elsewhere. Big engines were the order of the day. We have already encountered its three 2-8-0s built in 1906 and 1907, but only three years later three magnificent 0-6-6-0 Mallets arrived from Atlas of Stockholm. They remained the principal locos for the remainder of the steam era. Here no 12 (Atlas 114/1910) crosses the River Jädraån, a little to the north west of Tallås, on 22 July 2006 on what is now the Jädraås-Tallås Järnväg, a heritage operation on a 6.5km section of the old line.

DONJ abandoned its passenger services in 1959. Like BLJ and NKIJ it was never nationalised. The Linghed-Jädraås section closed on 30 September 1968 and the last timber train from Jädraås ran on 2 October 1970, leaving just a short section at Norrsundet which was converted to standard gauge and handed over to SJ in 1971. The society which now runs JTJ was founded in 1961 in Gävle as the 891-Järnvägarnas Museisällskap. DONJ allowed them access to the railway in 1967 when it was already clear that it would soon close. When this happened the old owning company generously made them a gift of the Jädraås-Tallås section, the whole of the Jädraås workshops and engine shed complex and various pieces of motive power and rolling stock. One of them was this 4-wheeled steam railcar named MAJORN (Atlas 18/1888). She is a compound machine and, like NKIJ no 1, has a vertical boiler. The driver sits at the passenger end and only the fireman occupies the boiler compartment. MAJORN's main jobs included distributing wages and transporting the company doctor. Her name means "major" and the railcar was named after a director of DONJ's owing company who served in the army reserve. On 22 July 2006 she spent much of her day at Pallanite station, midway along the line, but her helpful crew ran her up and down the loop there for my benefit under the watchful eye of the stationmaster. Pallanite is a Finnish name and reflects immigration to the district in the seventeenth century at a time when Finland formed a part of Sweden.

HUPPEN, or TJIPPEN, is an even smaller vertical-boilered steam railcar or inspection vehicle which was designed by JA Westerlund, DONJ's traffic manager and built at Jädraås workshops in 1898. The intention was to use her instead of MAJORN when only one person needed to go out along the line. She has only one cylinder and so can sometimes be stuck in deadlock, but is light enough for the driver to be able to push her to get her going! Here she stands outside Jädraås engine shed on 22 July 2006. She was included in the 1971 gift to JTJ by the old company, along with another inspection vehicle which was converted in 1938 from an Austin 10 car to replace an earlier Scania-built machine. JTJ's collection also includes a petrol-driven inspection vehicle with a wooden body. It was built in the 1910s by Petrus Wikström, a driver on the Ågbanan, a little line which joined DONJ at Vintjärn. Mr Wikström used HUPPEN as a model for his creation and apart from the petrol engine in place of the boiler she looks remarkably similar. She can be coupled to a 2-wheeled trailer, possibly Sweden's only single-axle railway vehicle!

One of the JTJ society's objectives was to preserve locos and rolling stock from NKIJ, BLJ and the Ågbanan as well as its core collection of DONJ material. This 0-6-0T is BLJ no 8 (Motala 273/1901), one of the three locos which worked on in internal service at Långshyttan after the 1964 closure. She is considerably larger than KLOSTER, the loco now at the Långshyttan museum, and began life as no 4 of the Ulricehamns Järnväg where she ran alongside its three Fletcher Jennings 0-6-0STs including STEN STURE, the loco currently in pieces at Skara. When UJ was converted to standard gauge she was bought by the Ljungbyholm–Karlslunda Järnväg as their no 4 along with no 2 BOGESUND, another of its Fletcher Jennings locos. BOGESUND only lasted until 1914 but no 4, later renumbered 41, stayed on until moving to BLJ in 1939. At JTJ she carries her old UJ number and I was told that her blue paint is believed to represent her UJ livery. Here she sets off from Pallanite for Tallås on 22 July 2006. The two leading coaches are summer cars nos 204 and 205, built at Jädraås works in 1907 to cater for the railway's burgeoning tourist traffic. They were withdrawn in the 1940s and used for storage in the carpentry shops at the works. When they were restored in the 1980s traces of several early colourful liveries were found, and different ones were adopted for each of them. The third coach, DONJ no 215, is a conventional closed 4-wheeled coach built at Jädraås works in 1901.

By the time no 8 was withdrawn at Långshyttan in 1972 she had become Sweden's last narrow gauge steam loco in commercial service. JTJ paid more to buy her than they expected as they had to compete against others when BLJ's remaining locos were put up for sale. No 4 poses on the turntable at Tallås on 22 July 2006. This delightfully rural station boasts an attractive wooden building which dates from 1880, and former stables which now house the Café Mallet – what else could this eatery be called?! The station was the terminus of the heritage railway until 2000 when it was extended for rather more than 1km to Svartbäcken Nedre, at a point from which a forestry track has been built along the old route which blocks any further extension. Although BLJ's older locos, including its 0-6-0Ts, were given names, the railway had abandoned the practice by the time no 8 arrived. JTJ named her SIGBJÖRN, after Sigbjörn Holgersson, DONJ's manager who was especially helpful in arranging the gift of the railway and stock to them.

The Ågbanan's tiny loco no 2 KORSÅN (Falun 21/1902) was the one which was her builder's only 891mm gauge 0-6-0T but in 1908 she was fitted with a trailing truck. She weighs just 11½ tonnes and is fitted with an unusual variant of Walschaerts valve gear in which the expansion link is located well behind the driving axle. KORSÅN worked on the Ågbanan until it closed in 1948, and in the following year was sold to the Dannemora quarry. She was another gift to what became the JTJ society. After extensive restoration she first ran again on DONJ in 1967, soon after they were given access to the railway, and has generally been kept in working order ever since. On 22 July 2006 she was standing in Jädraås engine shed. The Ågbanan also had a 0-6-0T no 1, built by Kristinehamn in 1883, which worked for only three more years after being transferred to the quarry at Vintjärn in 1918, and a O&K 0-4-0T no 3 which came secondhand in 1918. They were both scrapped in 1950. JTJ also has a tiny 4-wheeled coach built in 1883 for the Ågbanan by Skabo, a Norwegian carriage builder.

Mariestad-Kinnekulle Järnväg's 2-4-0T no 6 (Motala 196/1898) was lurking at one end of Jädraås engine shed on 14 July 2016. MKJ was taken over by VGJ in 1909 and she became their no 22. She moved to BLJ in 1941 as their no 9 and was used mostly for shunting until the 1964 closure. She is another loco which went on to shunt at the Kloster ironworks at Långshyttan after the line was closed, and was sold to JTJ in 1969. Her pale green paint may have been an undercoat, as shortly afterwards she was painted dark green with much lining out, which was perhaps her original MKJ livery. The loco behind her was built as the Östra Smålands Järnväg's no 101 (Kalmar 7/1927) for shunting and working light freight trains and was Kalmar's first diesel. After SJ took over ÖSmJ in 1940 she became Zp class no 143 and shunted at Oskarhamn harbour before being sold to DONJ in 1960. The diesels serving DONJ were generally painted orange with green cabs but the colours were mistakenly reversed on this loco and she has stayed that way ever since. DONJ seems never to have numbered her. Its first diesels, nos 1-4, were supplied by ASJ in 1959 and were all scrapped in 1973. SJ did not love the two T2p machines it inherited from SRJ and hired them to DONJ from 1964 until it closed, after which they too were scrapped. Z4p class nos 311 and 329 came secondhand from SJ in 1966 as nos 5 and 6; no 5 is now at JTJ, which later acquired two more Z4p locos, SJ no 321 and NKIJ no 2, the latter arriving there after a spell with Roslagsbanan.

In the early evening of 22 July 2006 no 12's work is over and she is slowly backing into Jädraås engine shed. Space is so tight there for this huge loco that she can only fit in with her tender coupling overhanging a rear window cill! Out of these three magnificent machines built in 1910, nos 1, 8 and 12, only no 1 failed to survive, being scrapped in 1961. No 8 was included in the 1971 gift to JTJ. She had become DONJ's last steam loco when she stopped work in 1966, but was steamed again to head the last timber train from Jädraås on 2 October 1970. The 1959-built diesels were intended to replace the Mallets, but they were puny in comparison, and it needed three of them to haul the same load! No 8 was stored out of use when I first visited in 2006 but as I write this is undergoing a major overhaul with much of the work being done offsite. No 12 went to Järnvägsmuseet in 1967 and has been at Jädraås on loan since 1983. Thanks to the generosity of DONJ's management back in 1971, as well as the dedicated work of many volunteers, JTJ is a truly superb heritage railway and one that is well worth travelling a very long way to visit.

This cumbersome-looking loco (Nohab 72/1876), which I saw on 13 July 2016, was the younger of two 762mm gauge 0-4-2Ts at Iggesund ironworks, on Sweden's Baltic coast about 300km north of Stockholm. A new boiler was built for her at Gävle in 1927. When her sister, which was two years older, expired in 1943 she took her number and the O&K 0-4-0T which replaced her became no 2. There was also a no 3, another O&K 0-4-0T which arrived in 1924. The 0-4-2Ts' design owed much to the dispute between Claes Adelsköld and Harald Asplund over their rival rear carrying wheel designs. Asplund designed FÖRSTLINGEN and the Frykstad loco for Munktells before going on to found the Kristinehamn factory, whereas Adelsköld licensed his radial axle to Nohab. He designed the Iggesund locos and some of their unusual characteristics resulted from the need to avoid any breach of Asplund's patents. They included a marine-type circular firebox to accommodate his radial axle with its large carrying wheels, which in this case were the same size as the drivers, rather than Asplund's long and wide firebox. The arrangement proved ideal for maintaining high pressure in a very narrow gauge loco as CE Spooner had advised. After retiring in 1948 the loco took up residence in the main ironworks hall, built of some of the largest stone blocks I have ever seen. This establishment had the unusual distinction of having been destroyed by the naval forces of Tsar Peter the Great of Russia in 1721 - and maybe those huge blocks were intended to make sure this would never again! In later years the business was noted for producing saw blades, chisels and stone- and mine-implements. The railway, 8.5kms long, was used mainly to bring in timber for the furnaces and ran from 1874 until 1955, when the O&Ks were scrapped.

What a delightful little loco! 0-6-0T LOKE (Kristinehamn 45/1887) sets off on the sunny evening of 13 July 2016 along the short branch serving her engine shed at the Galtströms Bruksmuseum, near the Baltic coast about 60kms north of Iggesund. The museum occupies what remains of another small ironworks and when it was founded back in 1673 it was the first in Medelpad. Its manager's house was another victim of Peter the Great's activities in 1721. The first section of the railway was built in the 1860s between the ironworks and Prästviken harbour, a short distance to the east. In 1877 it was extended to Utterviken, a better harbour over a headland about 2km to the north, and also inland towards woods in order to transport timber for fuel at the furnaces and to serve a sawmill and the rolling mills. In its new form it was about 3.2km long, and was horse-worked until LOKE arrived. Iron ore from Bergslagen, limestone from Roslagen and quartz from the Stockholm archipelago were brought in by sea for the furnaces and iron was shipped out. The Galtström ironworks was bought by the Kloster concern in 1873 and according to some reports LOKE may have worked first at their Born works before moving north, but others say she was shipped direct from Kristinehamn to Utterviken by boat. She is rated at 15hp and her maximum speed is 20kph. The railway closed in about 1932 and LOKE was its only locomotive. The Iggesund and Galtström businesses, like the one at Delary and others elsewhere in Sweden, successfully made the transition from iron to paper-making, using their extensive forests as a resource, once small-scale iron production became uneconomic.

On 13 July 2016 LOKE crosses the bridge over the River Armsjö, on the old line inland from Galtström, after taking water there. The ironworks tower is to the right. I was told that the loco only ever had one driver, Mr Johan Albert Nyström, who maintained her in pristine condition. After the closure he worked hard to ensure her survival, initially by dismantling the branch leading to her shed so that the scrapmen could not use her. He kept the key and made surreptitious visits to keep her in good shape. She became an exhibit when the Bruksmuseum was set up in 1955 and in 1990 a small group of enthusiasts began to restore her to working order. Her boiler and some platework are new but otherwise she contains all her original parts. It wasn't difficult to ascertain what her old paint scheme was since she has never been painted in any other way! The group has rebuilt about 2.4km of the old line, running from the woods and past the ironworks to Utterviken, where several of its members are also involved in a volunteer-run maritime museum. In 2014 OPHELIA, a tugboat which was built for Galtström in 1885 but spent most of her life elsewhere, returned to Utterviken after many years out if use, and has become a major restoration project. LOKE is not quite the northernmost working steam loco in the Swedish-speaking world as the little Nykarleby Järnväg, which operates some fascinating 600mm gauge industrial locos over on the other side of the Gulf of Bothnia in a part of Finland where most people are of Swedish origin, is a little further north, but for authenticity she is definitely in a league of her own!

The 3ft 6ins Setesdalsbanen opened in 1896 and ran for 78kms northwards from Kristiansand, a major port on Norway's south coast, to Byglandsfjord. It was isolated from the national network for many years until the standard gauge railway being built from Oslo to Stavanger reached its station at Grovane, 11kms north of Kristiansand, in 1938, and took over its route to Kristiansand. Setesdalsbanen was cut back to Grovane and a new loco depot, workshops and transhipment facilities were built there. Conversion of Norway's 3ft 6ins gauge main lines to standard gauge began in 1909. It was completed when Vestfoldbanen, which serves the district south west of Drammen, was rebuilt in 1949, leaving only some minor or isolated lines which were deemed to have no long-term future, to remain narrow gauge to the end. They included Setesdalsbanen, which had become NSB's last narrow gauge railway by the time it closed in 1962. Two Danish enthusiasts, supported by the Danish Locomotive Club, took the initiative in suggesting that a part of it should be preserved. They found sympathetic ears in the local NSB management and the district's tourist authorities. A preservation society was set up and the 5km line north from Grovane as far as Beihølen reopened in June 1964. On 24 August 2008 2-4-2T no 6 (Thunes 7/1901) and 2-6-2T no 5 (Thunes 4/1901) emerge from Grovane engine shed.

Since 1996 the heritage railway has been extended northwards from Beihølen and it reached Røyknes station, 8km from Grovane, in 2004. On 24 August 2008 no 5 has just left Beihølen station. It lies close to a dam which forms part of a hydro-electric scheme, and the rest of the run to Røyknes is alongside the reservoir. The railway offers a most attractive ride. Over the years Setesdalsbanen became home to rolling stock displaced from other lines as they were closed or converted to standard gauge. The leading coach is one of four generally similar vehicles built in 1908 by Skabo for Thamshavnbanen, a privately-run metre gauge line near Trondheim which has always been electrified. Its passenger service ended in 1963 and it closed altogether in 1974. The coach was regauged and presented to Setesdalsbanen three years later. More recently most of Thamshavnbanen has reopened as a heritage railway and its other three coaches are again in use there. The other vehicles in this train date from NSB's 3ft 6ins days.

No 5 returns to Grovane with a short train on 24 August 2008. The line in the foreground leads to the 1938 loco depot and workshops, and also to a carriage shed built in matching style by the preservation society. Further up the valley beyond Røyknes many of the old buildings survive, while the imposing station building at Kristiansand is still very much in use and now serves the main line trains. After Setesdalsbanen closed NSB sold several of its coaches to Sulitjelmabanen, a privately-owned railway north of the Arctic Circle near Bodø, which served a copper mining district. It started out in 1892 as a 750mm gauge line about 13km long, worked by two 0-4-0Ts which were little bigger than shunting locos, primarily to carry the copper pyrites, though of necessity there was also a passenger service since there was no other access to Sulitjelma. The pyrites made a complicated journey which involved shipping them from the mines to the railway over one lake, and again from the railway's far end over another. In 1915 the line was extended to reach the mines and was converted to 3ft 6ins. In 1955 it was extended again to reach a junction with the NSB Nordland main line at Finneid, close to its northern terminus at Bodø, and the railway reached its maximum lenth of 33km. Much of the final extension consisted of long tunnels, and the railway was then 33km long. After Sulitjelmabanen closed in 1972 the ex-NSB coaches returned to Setesdalsbanen, by then a heritage operation, and a diesel railcar also went there. The last mine at Sulitjelma closed in 1991 after the operation became financially unviable. There are still large untapped deposits of pyrites in the district.

The steam locos on Setesdalsbanen are peculiar, with a wheelbase which looks too long for the superstructure. Their design resulted from the need to keep their axle-loading under five tonnes, remarkably low for these sizeable machines, and to cope with the line's one hundred metre radius curves and steep gradients. Soon after they were built they were fitted with spark arresters which are so large that they require stays up from the smokebox to keep them in place – adding still further to their unusual appearance. They are not at all typical of most of NSB's 3ft 6ins gauge locos. Here no 5 emerges from a rock cutting near Grovane on her way to Røyknes on 24 August 2008.

Four locos were purchased from Dübs of Glasgow for Setesdalsbanen's opening in 1896. Nos 1 and 2 (NSB's type XXI) were 2-6-2T's intended for freight services and nos 3 and 4 (type XXII) were 2-4-2T passenger locos. Nos 1 and 2 still exist and here no 2 was undergoing major overhaul in the Grovane workshops on 24 August 2008, while no 1, on loan from the Norsk Jernbanemuseum at Hamar, was stored at the back of the engine shed. The locos successfully coped with the line's demanding requirements. Nos 5 and 6 were direct copies of them and no 7, a final 2-6-2T built by Hamar Jernstøberi in 1912, was similar to the earlier ones except that her cylinders were larger. She was the only 2-6-2T not to survive. Type XXVI 2-6-4T no 81 has recently arrived on loan from the Hamar museum. She is one of two locos built by Hamar Jernstøberi in 1915 to assist southbound trains from Langlete over a steep hill on the Rørosbanen. After it was converted to standard gauge in 1941 the two type XXVIs were transferred to Drammen for service on Vestfoldbanen in its final narrow gauge years. Petrol-engined railcars were introduced in the 1930s and took over most passenger services. Nos 3 and 4, the two Dübs 2-4-2T's, were scrapped, but fortunately no 6 was spared. The preservation society bought former SJ Z4t diesel no 307 in 1976 and her sister no 227 in 1981. They are the only surviving locos from Sweden's 3ft 6ins gauge system apart from the 4-4-0T at Kristianstad and the 2-6-0 at Gävle. They are very much in use for work trains and shunting.

Three other second-hand locos once ran on Setesdalsbanen but they all disappeared well before the closure. Numbers 13 and 64 were 2-6-2T's. To British eyes the third, no 87, formerly no 3 HARALD of Drammen-Randsfjordbanen, is of particular interest. She was one of twenty five type IV 2-4-0T's and was built by Beyer Peacock in 1867. We think of them as being Isle of Man-type locos. However the first Manx ones were built in 1873 whereas the type had been running in Norway since 1866, and the original Beyer Peacock works drawings which are still kept at Douglas are headed "Norwegian Narrow Gauge Tank". They resulted from a decision by Mr Pihl, the originator and champion of the Norwegian narrow gauge who became director of the state railways in 1865, that his system should have purpose-designed locos. The design was derived from the standard gauge 4-4-0T's which they were building for London's Metropolitan Railway, like the one now at the London Transport Museum at Covent Garden. No 87 only ran on Setesdalsbanen from 1922 to 1925 and was scrapped in 1927. No type IV loco has survived in Norway but here is type V 2-4-0T HUGIN (Motala 43/1881) in the booking hall at Stavanger station on 13 October 2008. The ten type Vs were generally similar to the type IVs save that they were built to metric measurements. HUGIN ran as no 1 on the Bergen-Voss line until it was converted to standard gauge in 1904 and she was transferred to Flekkefjordbanen, west of Kristiansand, becoming its no 10. Her final duties were to work the short branch between the old and new stations at Egersund between 1944 and 1949. In 2014 she moved to the Hamar museum.

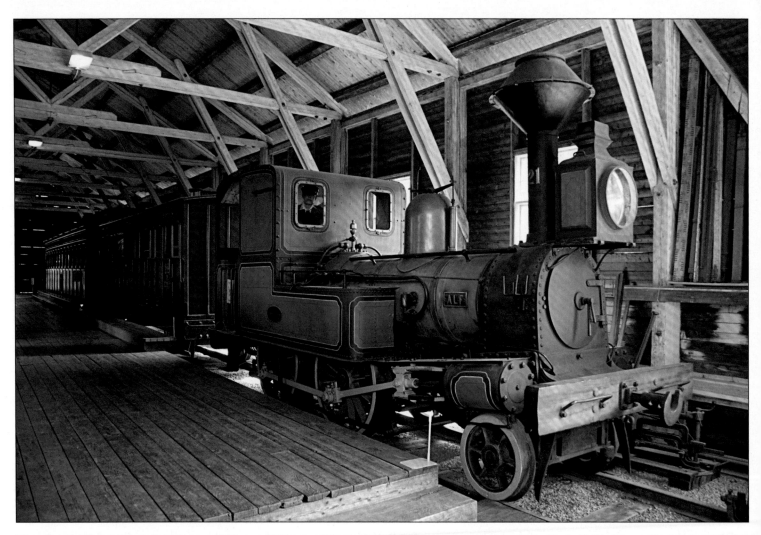

The six type III 2-4-0Ts built between 1868 and 1871 were the smallest of NSB's locos with a weight of just 13.2 tonnes. No 4 (later 21) ALF (BP 992/1870) worked initially on Hamar-Grundsetbanen, the southernmost section of Rørosbanen and the first public 3ft 6ins line anywhere in the world when it opened in 1862. The type proved too small for many services and four of the six ended up on Flekkefjordbanen and on Jærbanen, effectively Flekkefjordbanen's extension northwards from Egersund which provided a through route between Flekkefjord and Stavanger. The last type III there worked until 1934, but ALF retired in 1923 after spending all her working life on Rørosbanen. She has been at the Hamar museum since 1928, and still carries the paint applied during her final overhaul in 1915. The second carriage of her short train is a royal saloon which on one occasion was used to convey King Chulalongkorn, Thailand's great modernising monarch who oversaw construction of his country's early railways. It was built by Jackson and Sharp at Wilmington, Delaware in 1877 and is similar to one previously supplied to Emperor Don Pedro II of Brazil. It was NSB's first bogie and first corridor vehicle. An unusual feature of Norway's 3ft 6ins carriages was that the gangway between them was positioned to one side instead of centrally, and so they all needed to be orientated the same way on each line. SJ bought some second hand in the late 1940s for its 3ft 6ins lines and had to rebuild them with conventional ends. On 4 June 2008 ALF stood in a building which is termed the carriage hall at the museum but which is also used to house its collection of 3ft 6ins gauge locos. The similarity between the type IIIs and the larger type IVs like the Isle of Man locos is clear for all to see. What a very pretty loco!

This very stylish type XIII 2-cylinder compound 4-4-0 was Flekkefjordbanen's no 7 (Thunes 1/1900). Thirteen type XIIIs were built, four by Dübs between 1893 and 1895, three by Hartmann between 1895 and 1900 and the final two by Thunes in 1900 and 1902, and no 7 was one of the last three in service. They were all withdrawn in 1946. The Thunes locos were distinctive with their US-style wooden cabs, whereas the Dübs and Hartmann ones had conventional steel ones. No 7 was chosen for preservation as the first loco built by Thunes, which went on to be Norway's most prolific constructor. Here she is at the Hamar museum on 4 June 2008. The type XIIIs also worked on Rørosbanen and on Randsfjordbanen. They were developed from four type XI simple 4-4-0s built by Dübs in 1881, and one each of types XII and XIIa by Nohab ten years later, both compounds. When Flekkefjordbanen and Jærbanen became a part of the standard gauge Oslo-Stavanger line in 1944 a new station was built in the outskirts of Egersund, and the line to the old station in the town centre became the short branch on which HUGIN worked out her last years. The Flekkefjord end of the railway was also excluded from the standard gauge main line and became another branch. It was included in the gauge conversion but retained its previous loading gauge which required special rolling stock, latterly in the shape of some ex-SJ Y6 railcars until it closed in 1990. It is rather ironic that two locos from this relatively insignificant little railway, as well as ALF, from a type long associated with it, should be amongst the very few 3ft 6ins ones to have survived in Norway.

0-4-0T LOKE (Hanomag 2411/1892), the only other 3ft 6ins gauge machine at the Hamar museum, was Sulitjelmabanen's first loco. Her sister TYR arrived in 1893, and Hartmann-built 0-6-0T ODIN in 1904, similar to their first two locos for Tertitten (see below) but with longer tanks. TYR was withdrawn in 1915 but LOKE and ODIN were converted to 3ft 6ins. Hartmann built two more 3ft 6ins 0-6-0Ts in 1914, named SAULO and SULITJELMA. Three secondhand locos came in the 1950s, a 0-4-0T also named TYR and two ex-Vestfoldbanen type XXIII 2-6-0s. Their arrival enabled LOKE to be withdrawn in 1952. Loke is the name of a god in Norse mythology who was associated with fire and magic, appropriate perhaps for both her and her equally remote namesake at Galtström! She worked again briefly in 1956 and 1957 and was presented to the Hamar museum in 1962. On 4 June 2008 she was tucked away in a dark corner of the old carriage shed beyond the royal saloon in ALF's train, lit mostly from behind. I wished I had brought a flashgun, but I hope this photo conveys something of her character. It's a shame that she has lost her connecting rod! In its last years Sulitjelmabanen was diesel-worked. The main reason for its closure in 1972 was to enable a road to be built through the long tunnels on the 1955 extension and on to Sulitjelma to connect the village to the national network for the first time. Previously road vehicles could only reach it via a railway piggyback service. Road traffic began only three weeks after the last train ran, although the construction work wasn't finished until 1975. It was a sad end to what must have been a magnificent railway.

"Tertitten" is the Norwegian word for "Tertiary", and under Norway's railway classification system it means a lightly constructed line, often an insignificant one. The part of Setesdalsbanen north of Grovane was one of these. Urskog-Hølandsbanen was another and it was probably its insignificance which allowed it to adopt the 750mm gauge at a time when the country was looking towards building a unified, standard gauge system. The first section opened in 1896 between a junction with NSB's Kongsvinger main line at Bingsfos and Bjørkelangen, the only town of any size along the route. Two years later it was extended southwards to Skulerud, and in 1903 a final 2km section opened from Bingsfos to Sørumsand which became the main line junction. It started out with two Hartmann-built 0-6-0T's. No. 1 was scrapped as early as 1924 but no 2 (Hartmann 2102/1895), latterly named URSKOG, lasted in service until 1954 as NSB's class XXVII. The railway closed in 1960, after which URSKOG and 2-6-2T no 7 PRYDZ were transferred to the Hamar museum along with three carriages. A short demonstration railway opened in 1962, worked at first by PRYDZ, but URSKOG took over in 1982 and has run there ever since. Here she is midway along the line on 4 June 2008. The leading coach, UHB no 4, was one of two which came from Skabo when the Skulerud extension opened in 1898. The second one, no 8, was built by Skabo in 1914, and no 9 behind it by the Oldbury RC&W Company in 1895, both for Nesstun-Osbanen near Bergen, Norway's first tertiary railway. They were bought by UHB after it closed in 1935. NOB was a Decauville-inspired line, complete with three Mallet tanks like LESSEBO. I thought that coach no 8 greatly resembled the Decauville ones on ÖSlJ.

Hartmanns were able to submit a low tender to build nos 1 and 2 as they already had an order for two similar locos for Lillesand-Flaksvatnbanen, an isolated 3ft 6ins line near Kristiansand, and so benefitted from economies of scale. By the time the Skulerud extension opened in 1898 there was an urgent need for a third loco. European builders had full order books and the order for the new machine, 2-6-2 no 3 HØLAND, went to Baldwin in Philadelphia. She wasn't particularly successful and was scrapped in 1924, but the railway must have appreciated the 2-6-2T concept as it remained faithful to it for all its later locos – and returned to Hartmann to build them until the firm went out of business in 1930. During a heavy overhaul in 2009 and 2010 URSKOG was modified to run on agricultural bio-pellets, and must now be as carbon-friendly as it is possible for a steam loco to be! Here she approaches the eastern terminus on 7 July 2010. The elaborate and delightful wooden station building on the left dates from 1893 and is very typical of Norwegian design at that time. It came from Ilseng, on the Rørosbanen between Hamar and Støren. On the right is the old carriage hall where the museum's 3ft 6ins locos live, and an extension houses the magnificent standard gauge class 49c 2-8-4 no 470, built by Krupp in 1940. She is one of the country's largest passenger locos, which were generally called "Dovregubben" after a character in Henrik Ibsen's play "Peer Gynt".

A preservation society for the Tertitten railway was started in 1961. It began services five years later from a station in the outskirts of Sørumsand, through Bingsfos and on up the steep hill to Fossum, a 2% grade with 100m radius curves. The access at Sørumsand, a small town about 30km north east of Oslo, was far from satisfactory. The local authority wanted to use the line's old route into the town to extend the town's car parking facilities and for many years vigorously resisted reinstatement of the line towards the NSB station. Permission was eventually obtained, the track was relaid and services began in 1987, giving the railway a total route of about 4km. On 19 August 2007 no 4 SETSKOGEN (Hartmann 3356/1909), the first of the four generally similar 2-6-2Ts, was the loco in use. Here she is about to pass under a section built in 1862 of Kongsvingerbanen, in the eastern outskirts of Sørumsand. In 1871 Kongsvingerbanen was extended to Charlottenberg, just over the border in Sweden, to form Norway's first connection with the Swedish system. Nowadays it forms a part of the main line between Oslo and Stockholm, though there are no longer any express services on the Norwegian section – very odd considering the emphasis which both countries now place on their green credentials. Most remarkably two of the line's original 2-4-0s, both built by Robert Stephenson in 1861, survive at the Hamar museum. More remarkably still one of them is in working order and makes regular excursions with a train of period carriages, often over what was once the narrow gauge Hamar-Grundsetbanen where ALF ran when she was new.

It was a dark, snowy and bitterly cold evening when I arrived at Sørumsand on 10 December 2010. I should have been there much earlier but my flight from the UK was delayed by exceptionally cold weather in Norway. Even the sea in the Oslofjord had frozen! The last train of the day was about to leave and I was glad to be able to climb up into the warmth of the old wooden carriage. The guard was surprised that anyone should have come from abroad to visit his railway in such extreme conditions. After the train returned to Sørumsand he invited me into his office where a huge log fire awaited, and spent a long time poring over the society's stock of old publications to find some material in English - a really kind person. I woke up the next morning to find there had been more snow overnight, though by then the sky was clear – and if anything the temperature was even colder. PRYDZ (Henschel 28463/1950), which returned to the railway from the Hamar museum in 1987 on loan, was the working loco. She was raising steam in the engine shed before working the day's services as SETSKOGEN stood on the right. The loco beyond her is 2-6-2T no 6 HØLAND (Hartmann 4658/1925). The fourth of these locos, no 5 BJÖRKELANGEN, is preserved at the University of Science and Technology at Trondheim. The spelling of its name is unusual as it uses the Swedish Ö to represent the long O sound instead of the Norwegian Ø.

PRYDZ has ventured out of the shed and approaches the frozen water column at Sørumsand station before working the day's first train on 11 December 2010. She was the last steam loco of any gauge to be added to NSB's stock. They did not normally give their locos names, but made a well-deserved exception with no 7 when they named her after Mr Eigil Prydz, Tertitten's general manager from 1916 until 1951. The railway led a hand to mouth existence for many years and probably owed its survival to him. It's said that at times there was so little cash that Mr Prydz would pedal his bike each evening to a local farmer and use the day's takings to buy enough wood to fire up the loco the next day. By 1939 the line had become Norway's last remaining private railway. The years of the German occupation of Norway during the Second World War were particularly difficult and Mr Prydz was able to arrange for NSB to take it over in 1945.

PRYDZ approaches Fossum station, the far terminus of the preserved railway, on 11 December 2010 as suitably seasonal connecting transport awaits! I'd stopped to buy sandwiches from a supermarket in Sørumsand the previous evening for my lunch, kept them in the fridge in my hotel room overnight and stowed them in the back of my hire car in the morning - but when I came to eat them after taking this photo they had frozen solid!

The railway's 4km length may not sound much but there is some attractive and varied scenery to be enjoyed. In this photo PRYDZ runs down the hill between Fossum and Bingsfos on 11 December 2010 along with the railway's collection of period carriages. The one nearest the loco was built by Skabo in 1912 for Sulitjelmabanen in its 750mm gauge days, and became a 3ft 6ins vehicle after the railway's gauge was converted only three years later. It was a considerable advance on any previous Norwegian 750mm carriage, and was converted back to 750mm after it was presented to Tertitten following the 1972 closure. The two short coaches in the middle of the train were built for UHB's opening in 1896 and the longer ones for the Skulerud extension in 1898.

A final view of PRYDZ, this time after she had arrived at Fossum on 11 December 2010. None of the old buildings survived on the preserved railway, save that the old Sørumsand station building still serves the NSB trains there. The society has built some from scratch as replicas and relocated others from further along the old line. The building at Fossum was moved from Mork, a short distance to the south, and is typical of those which served the railway's small stations. Particularly impressive replicas are the new station building, the loco shed and the works at Sørumsand, all based on originals which stood at Bjørkelangen. Their construction was needed as UHB never had any facilities of its own at Sørumsand. After taking these photos I returned to my hotel near Sørumsand hoping for an early supper but, alas, its restaurant was closed. Sunday evenings are not a good time to be eating out in much of Norway but happily a Thai restaurant just along the road was open. I had spent the previous weekend in Bangkok and so was familiar with the fare on offer, but didn't expect to be sampling it again quite so soon, and definitely not in such contrasting climatic conditions!

The land of the midnight sun, save that on 21 July 2008 the sun was, at best, hazy! Ny Ålesund, in north western Svalbard, is the world's most northerly permanently-occupied settlement at a latitude of 79 degrees, and lies just 1,231km from the North Pole. 900mm gauge 0-4-0T no 2 (Borsig 7095/1909) and her train stand next to Kongsfjorden, with the Kongsbreen glacier as a backdrop. Coal from Svalbard became vital to Norway during the First World War when imports from the UK, its traditional source, were embargoed. The Ny Ålesund collieries and their railway operated from 1917 until they closed in 1963 after twenty one miners were killed in an underground explosion. By then they were state-owned, and the disaster led to the collapse of the Norwegian government. Three 891mm locos came from NOJ and VJ and some have suggested that maybe this was the true gauge. My wife and I took a tape measure with us to check, and it is definitely 900mm! During this visit we had the company of an arctic fox, who decided we were his friends, and arctic terns, extraordinarily aggressive birds which like to divebomb their targets, which on this occasion included us! There are many "most northerlies" here including the post office, the North Pole Hotel and the disused collieries as well as the train. No 2 was built for a steelworks at Zabrze in Silesia, then part of Germany but now in southern Poland. She moved to a colliery at Salangsverket in northern Norway, and was Ny Ålesund's first loco when she arrived on 12th July 1917. In 2016 she made the long journey to Tertitten's workshops at Sørumsand for a makeover but is now back in her chilly northern home!

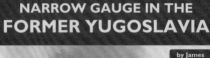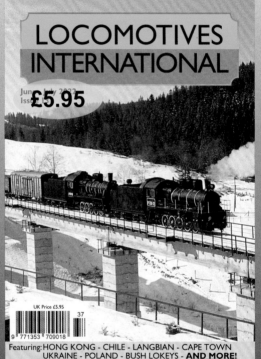